UNLOCKING THE NATURAL-BORN LEADER'S ABILITIES

An Autobiographical Exposé

UNLOCKING THE NATURAL-BORN LEADER'S ABILITIES

An Autobiographical Exposé

Salar A. Khan, MD, MBA

Library of Congress Control Number: 2017904394
ISBN: Hardcover   978-1-5245-9956-0
               Softcover   978-1-5245-9957-7
               eBook   978-1-5245-9958-4

http://doctorsalarkhan.com

Rev. date: 08/08/2019

To order additional copies of this book, contact:
Xlibris
1-888-795-4274
www.Xlibris.com
Orders@Xlibris.com
755472

CONTENTS

To my late father, Mukhtar Ahmed Khan.

To my late mother, Noorjehan.

To my children, Faraz Ahmed Khan and Saad Ahmed Khan.

To my wife, Rubina Salar.

Disclaimer

This book will serve as a discussion on the natural-born leader through an autobiographical lens. It is not meant to be a book based on research, but it will rather present anecdotes from my life to substantiate what I think are the essential qualities and characteristics of a natural-born leader. I hope that by reading this book, you may, through introspection, potentially uncover these qualities within yourself.

There is some intentional repetition in prose about leadership learning process because most readers do not read book in one sitting. In my opinion repetition of some elements will provide a good continuity to grasp basic concepts related to leadership to become a confident leader. Anyone can be a leader either working in a big or smaller organization or any institution or even at home as one of parents to manage and guide kids or family members.

Book Review Mini-Critique

Below you will find ratings (scale of 1-5) with descriptions for the major parts of your book followed by your Readers' Favorite review. Although these are general ratings we hope they will give you an insight into how others may view the different components of your book. These are the opinions of your reviewer, and although your reviewer is not an expert literary critic or professional editor, they are at the very least, an avid reader of books just like yours.

Title: Unlocking the Natural-Born Leader's Abilities
Subtitle: An Autobiographical Expose
Author: Salar A. Khan, MD, MBA
Genre: Non-Fiction – Autobiography

Appearance: 5
The appearance of a book can make a significant impact on the experience of a reader, whose enjoyment is often enhanced by an enticing cover, an intriguing table of contents, interesting chapter headings, and when possible, eye-catching illustrations.

Plot: 5
The characters of a book should be well defined with strengths and flaws, and while they do not have to be likable, the reader does

have to be able to form a connection with them. The tone should be consistent, the theme should be clear, and the plot should be original or told from a unique perspective. For informative books -- those without plot and characters--this rating refers primarily to your concept and how well you presented it.

Development: 5

Development refers to how effectively you told your story or discussed your topic. The dialogue should be realistic, the descriptions should be vivid, and the material should be concise and coherent. Organization is also a key factor, especially for informative books -- those without plot and characters. The order in which you tell your story or explain your topic and how smoothly it flows can have a huge impact on the reader's understanding and enjoyment of the material.

Formatting: 5

Formatting is the single most overlooked area by authors. The way in which you describe scenes, display dialogue, and shift point of view can make or break your story. In addition, excessive grammatical errors and typos can give your book an amateurish feel and even put off readers completely.

Marketability: 4

Marketability refers to how effectively you wrote your book for your target audience. Authors may include content that is above or below the understanding of their target reader, or include concepts, opinions or language that can accidentally confuse or alienate some readers. Although by its nature this rating is very subjective, a very low rating here and poor reviews may indicate an issue with your book in this area.

Overall Opinion: 5

The overall starred rating takes into account all these elements and describes the overall reading experience of your reviewer. This is the official Readers' Favorite review rating for your book.

Review: Reviewed by Vincent Dublado for Readers' Favorite

What most natural-born leaders have in common is that they wield a resumé that highlights their impressive credentials reflective of their climb to success. Salar A. Khan, MD, MBA is no exception. But to label him as just another motivational author would be inaccurate. In Unlocking the Natural-Born Leader's Abilities: An Autobiographical Exposé, Salar Khan presents his thesis on the anatomy of natural-born leaders (NBLs) that runs in a motivational and autobiographical vein. His primary take on the concept of NBLs is that they are the types who do not seek extrinsic rewards but are rather motivated by an intrinsic sense of fulfillment. He presents himself as a case study with a healthy degree of objectivity and without narcissistic undertones. Unlike other avant-garde motivational authors, Salar Khan does not aim for a disputation of nature versus nurture. Rather, he subscribes to the imperative of unlocking people's leadership potential--a far more practical approach given that great leaders can come from anywhere. The narrative is engaging in that it appeals to a general audience. Unlocking the Natural-Born Leader's Abilities is worth your time because it will not tell you something that you already know. Instead, it inspires you to take action to accomplish your goals. It does not feed you with trite lecturings commonly found within the shibboleths of the motivation culture. The author even provides self-assessment tools to help his readers make a critical and objective analysis of their achievements and shortcomings. What is perhaps the most important nugget of truth that this book imparts is relating to readers what Salar Mr. Khan has effectively done not just in theory, but in practice.

KIRKUS
REVIEWS

A leadership guide with an autobiographical foundation.

In his nonfiction debut, Pakistan-born physician Khan lays out his concept of "natural-born leaders"—people who are "optimistic, selfless, and do not seek external rewards or glory," and instead seek "a sense of internal satisfaction and happiness." According to the author, such people are "target-oriented, fully focused, self-confident, and intrinsically motivated to accomplish their tasks," and the main goal of his book is to help his readers identify and enhance the natural-born leadership qualities inside themselves. Khan himself says that he "unlocked" his own leadership skills while working as an internist, pulmonologist, and chief of medicine in Saudi Arabia, but he says that he began the process in childhood, when he embraced responsibility and its rewards. The author takes readers through the various stages of his career in medicine, from residency to upper management, and draws lessons about self-confident leadership from a variety of trying circumstances—lessons that Khan asserts are crucial in the modern era, when the world is suffering from a "crisis when it comes to leadership"... Fortunately, the quality of the other major narrative strand of Khan's book—his personal experiences dealing with patients, fellow doctors, and supervisors over a career spanning half a century—more than compensates. Their behind-the-scenes glimpses of the medical world are consistently gripping, whether they demonstrate the "unlocking" of leadership traits or not.

Khan delivers a highly readable mixture of motivational manual and medical memoir.

EXCERPTING POLICIES

Please review Kirkus Media's excerpting policies before publishing any portion of this review online or in print for any use. To learn about proper attribution and to ensure your use is in compliance with our guidelines, we invite you to visit http://www.kirkusreviews.com/indieexcerpts. Kirkus Indie, Kirkus Media LLC, 6411 Burleson Rd., Austin, TX 78744 indie@kirkusreviews.com

Amazon Best Sellers Rank # 1

Author has permission from Editor "Self-Publishing Review" at Amazon to use all the following materials in the book.

"A unique and inspiring work
of leadership training."

★★★★

– Self-Publishing Review

"Khan writes with confidence, and with a gentle sense of humor. He seems to be able to look at himself as a subject of his story without undue ego, while still extolling the many skills that have gotten him to his place in life. Given the tumultuous path he has walked down, this book has much more to offer than the typical book on leadership, offering a unique and inspiring work of leadership training that can be used in both work and everyday life." Self-Publishing Review, ★★★★

Here is Author Interview, which is shared on social media:

https://www.selfpublishingreview.com/2019/01/an-interview-with-salar-a-khan-md-mba-author-of-unlocking-the-natural-born-leaders-abilities/

Please click above link then click "Book Review to read, then click "Blog" icon to open the following items one-by-one: lead story, book of week, and author interview.

By SPR|January 4th, 2019|Categories: Interviews|Tags: Salar A. Khan

Editor, SPR Amazon

Self Publishing Review

Lead Story

Lead stories from SPR's ever-growing independent book portal. The latest indie book reviews from Self-Publishing Review dated January 8, 2019. Categories: Book Reviews, Lead Story. Tags: Business, Leadership, Non-Fiction, Salar A. Khan.

Review: Unlocking the Natural-Born Leader's Abilities by Salar A. Khan, MD, MBA

A successful example of what he wishes to convey, award-winning author Salar Khan uses his own life as an illustration of what constitutes leadership in *Unlocking the Natural-Born Leader's Abilities: An Autobiographical Exposé*. Carefully presenting an objective picture, Khan shares his own memories to demonstrate the sorts of qualities a natural-born leader (NBL) would have, both innately and from training and experience.

Khan's early life was rigorous: His parents were forced to migrate from India to Pakistan a few years before he was born, and six of his eleven siblings died by the age of four. When he was eleven, his home city of Karachi was under air attack. His schooling began at the fifth-grade level after being homeschooled. In his spare time before classes he helped his mother with housework, and from her he learned about time and risk management.

Khan excelled in school, seemingly blessed with self-confidence, and at his father's advice, decided on a career in medicine. He became a doctor, a profession he felt he was born to. He worked as a pulmonologist in Saudi Arabia before making the bold step of immigrating to the US where initially he had to work at minimum wage jobs until obtaining an MBA for a new career. Throughout his career and personal life, he has successfully overcome negative dynamics, promoted positive outcomes, and won numerous professional awards in the US and internationally.

Khan expounds his belief that leadership begins in childhood with parental guidance through such methods as storytelling, and will increase over the course of one's life. He believes the NBL should have "an appreciation and understanding of as many perspectives and disciplines as possible." He or she should recognize and develop intuition, which he uses in the medical field to interpret nonverbal cues from his patients. He states that a basic store of knowledge builds insightfulness and reinforces intuition, a process that leads to self-confidence. He suggests that NBLs actually want to lead, and will take on that role without being asked. This in turn will cause others to look up to the NBL, and that admiration will be enhanced by the leader's capacity to communicate effectively at any level. He doesn't think the NBL needs any particular incentive to fulfill the role: "Power, money, beauty and health will not lead to happiness on their own."

As would be expected, Khan writes with confidence, and with a gentle sense of humor. He seems to be able to look at himself as a subject of his story without undue ego, while still extolling the many skills that have gotten him to his place in life. He provides useful charts and diagrams to underpin his points. The book ends with a simple, one-page self-assessment tool that the reader can use for exploring his or her own leadership qualities, including such simple statements as "I am insightful," and "I have fearlessness in making critical decisions."

Khan has walked the walk and now talks the talk, expressing his sincere wish that others might gain by his experience as a natural-born leader. Given the tumultuous path he has walked down, this book has much more to offer than the typical book on leadership, offering a unique and inspiring work of leadership training that can be used in both work and everyday life.

Author Interview

Interviews with indie authors, publishers and book service providers in the self-publishing realm

An Interview with Salar A. Khan, MD, MBA: Author of Unlocking the Natural-Born Leader's Abilities

Salar Ahmed Khan, MD, MBA, FACA, FCCP, DTCD, MCPS, worked as an internist and pulmonologist at Karachi, Pakistan, from 1985 to 1987; as the chief of medicine, the acting director of medical services, and acting hospital director at Al-Midhnab General Hospital under the Ministry of Health in Saudi Arabia from 1988 to 1993; as an associate professor of medicine at Baqai Medical College and Hospital in Karachi, Pakistan, from 1993 to 1994; as a surgical assistant, material management, and acting central processing supervisor at Edgewater Medical Center in Chicago from 1996 to 2000.

From 2000 to 2009, he was research administration portfolio manager, grant administrator, acting administrative officer, and acting director of a nonprofit organization, and since 2009 has been working as a director of research compliance in Chicago. He was nominated for and has won several awards at national and international levels. In his spare time, he enjoys cooking, photography, and watching sports such as cricket. He lives in Chicago with his wife and two sons.

Tell us about your book.

The book is *Unlocking the Natural-Born Leader's Abilities: An Autobiographical Exposé* – a leadership guide with an autobiographical foundation. The book received a couple of awards and delivers a highly readable mixture of motivational manual and medical memoir. Leadership is a habit we cultivate. It throws many challenges our way to rediscover who we are. While working under time-sensitive, high-risk, & high-pressure situations allowed me to unlock and develop my natural-born leader's abilities & find several potentially hidden skill-sets to become a successful self-confident leader during last fifty years. The book helps reader identify and enhance the natural-born leadership qualities inside themselves. With lessons embedded through the book and a self-assessment tool at the end, this book will set the blueprint to your success, ready to teach the art of successful leadership for the betterment of the world.

Why did you want to write a book?

This book is not based on research. It based on my observations and experience of life. Readers may introspect and potentially uncover the Natural Born Leader's Abilities (NBL) qualities within yourself. There is widespread lack of confidence in leadership – whether in business, govt, education, or elsewhere. Currently these organizations or institutions are managed by people who lack leadership competence. I believe the vision of self-confident NBL is necessary for the betterment of the world.

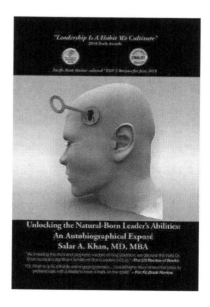

Why did you write about this particular subject?

This book is about my fifty-year journey to become a natural-born leader. I can be an NBL, why can't a reader of this book also be an NBL? This book is a leadership guide with an autobiographical foundation, which is a highly readable mixture of motivational manual and medical memoir.

Currently, there is a widespread lack of confidence in leadership – whether in business, government, education, or elsewhere. Leaders have fear of failure, and therefore, they cannot perform well. I believe the world is facing a crisis when it comes to leadership; our society needs more positive thinkers. We need the vision of a confident leader – that of an NBL is needed for the betterment of the world. This was my main motivation and inspiration for writing this book.

My observations and experiences throughout the last 50 years of my life also have served as an inspiration. I remembered my parents provided a foundation of achieving confidence by teaching me to set smaller tasks or targets in my daily life. Having a clear goal in mind is imperative for achieving success. Free to make self-decisions, analyzing mistakes, after achieving targets or goals feeling happy and self-rewarding yourself.

An incident made me realize how unpredictable life can really be. On Sunday, March 6, 2016, at about 6:00 PM, the thirty-six-year-old son of my elder sister was sitting on a carpet at home, working on his laptop. He had no history of any illness when, all of a sudden, he dropped dead on the carpet. There was no warning, no signs, and no symptoms. In two to three seconds, he had already departed. Life honestly doesn't play on anyone's timetable except its own. And so, I was compelled to start writing this book in December 2016.

Why did you choose to self-publish?

It was my first book. I was not aware about the book publication process. Now I've learned a lot about publication.

What tools or companies did you use, and what experience did you have?

I select one publication company Xlibris. It was an easygoing and very good experience. Editing and publication were completed in two months.

What tips can you give other authors looking to self-publish?

First, do your homework by finding a publishing company according to your needs. No publishing company is ideal. The decision to make about a publishing company for your book is always a gamble. Once you make a selection, be ready for surprises from time to time and paying more money. Everyone looks for their own benefits. I have no complaints.

What was your steepest learning curve during the publishing process?

Fortunately, I have a quick learning ability due to my positive attitude since childhood, confidence in my own abilities, and clarity of vision. I split my learning task into smaller component and focus to complete with efficient manner without any overwhelming feeling.

"A unique and inspiring work of leadership training."

As a writer, what is your schedule? How do you get the job done?

I am working full time as Director Research Compliance holding a top position at work. I have only weekends to think about writing book materials. Any time good thoughts come to my mind, I immediately write them down on paper and finalize the thought process during the weekend. I am very good with organization and time management since childhood, which helps me to organize my thoughts in a systematic fashion, giving me clear vision of how to prioritize my ideas. I think motivation and self-confidence are important to make the impossible possible. In this way anyone can accomplish a job on time.

How do you deal with writer's block?

This process is easy for me because of my profession as a physician and my superior management role. At work I am dealing with a lot of written materials, amounting to thousands of pages (in three years I reviewed 1.5 million pages of research documents). In this way my eyes are set how to scan materials or blocks quickly to understand hidden concepts. This habit has helped me reach quick solutions by analyzing important materials.

Tell us about the genre you wrote in, and why you chose to write this sort of book.

It is based on my observation and experiences over the last 50 years. I define NBL through an autobiographical lens. Throughout my career, I found myself working under time-sensitive, high-risk, and high-pressure situations, which allowed me to uncover and develop my NBL qualities. I learned through hardships and accepting challenges that have allowed me to become successful. It is my hope that perhaps some of the things I have learned can be useful to the reader.

Everyone possesses the essential qualities and abilities of NBL. It is simply a matter of bringing your hidden talents and skill sets to the surface. In my book, I identify the qualities and abilities of NBL, so they can be refined and perfected through education, training, and experience. NBL possess a unique ability to deal with stressful situations confidently – they are creative, knowledgeable and self-directed and often establish norms. And they are charismatic: the ability to inspire and motivate others to accomplish their goals with positive outcomes.

Many leaders choose to follow instead to lead due to fear of failure and unable to take risks, play safe, keep quiet when thing get worse. These leaders do not have trust on their own abilities. When leaders become followers, they make excuses and blame others for poor performance. My book can help leaders gain more confidence while performing a leadership role in any organization or institution. The book includes a self-assessment tool to evaluate your NBL abilities and identify where you ultimately fall on the spectrum.

Life isn't easy, but that's part of its charm. It throws many trials and suffering in our way to help us rediscover who we are. In doing so, we become stronger, more capable and in the process can help make the world a better place. The main goal of this book is to hopefully produce hundreds and thousands of confident leaders throughout the world either working in political, non- political, CEO in any organization, and even at individual level to make honest and sincere confident decisions on daily basis. Through my book, I want to generate a positive thinker class of people and true NBL in the world that leads to the prosperity of mankind and reduces negative thinking leaders or destructive type of leaders to avoid world crisis in the form of wars and a lot of human suffering. In my opinion, this world is a better place to live depending upon our world leaders, and which way they want to take this world.

In this way, we are losing great talent before they come to play their constructive role. Life is very short to do good things and to find new discoveries in every field of life for making paradise in this world. Always try to do good things and help humanity and try to reduce human suffering.

How do your friends and family get involved with your writing? What do they think of your book?

My two-medical college-going sons reviewed my book once I completed entire book and they thought that it is a good book based on my fifty years' experience and observation through my autobiographical lens. This is going to be a good educational book about leadership for readers.

What did you learn on your journey as an author?

After writing this book I gained more confidence that I can write another book, although English is my second language.

What's next for you as an author?

Next book coming soon: *Am I Burned out? A Self-Care Solution.*

OnlineBookClub.org

Post by mtsnel006 » 05 Nov 2018, 15:26

[Following is an official OnlineBookClub.org review of "Unlocking the Natural -Born Leader's Abilities: An Autobiographical Expose" by Salar A. Khan, MD, MBA.]

4 out of 4 stars "Unlocking the Natural -Born Leader's Abilities: An Autobiographical Expose" by Salar A. Khan, MD, MBA

Dr. Salar A. Khan in his book, Unlocking The Natural-Born Leader's Abilities: An Autobiographical Expose, shares what he has learned and experienced about leadership till the age of 62 years when he wrote this autobiography. Throughout his lifetime, Khan had played many roles, including the roles of being a tutor, doctor, chief of medicine, acting director of medical services, and acting administrative officer. It was by these roles that he became interested in leadership and ended up writing this book not based on research, but based on his autobiographical lens. He challenges several assumptions revolving around leadership, such as that "leaders are not born but are made." He asserts that everyone is born with enveloped qualities and abilities that make them natural-born leaders. In averting to start a disputation of nurture vs nature, he elaborates that inasmuch as everyone has the natural ability to lead, that ability needs to be harnessed and developed.

With this book, he focuses on fostering and unlocking the mindset of a natural leader to readers. Khan takes time to look back to his own life experiences for the readers to benefit from. He shares several occasions on how he helped other people and how that impacted on his life. He is very motivational in his books and tells the readers to be strong and not fear failure, but rather have self-confidence and strive for success. He does not say that natural-born leaders cannot fail, but that when they fail, they should fail fast so that that they can get back up again and carry on their journey. He even shares a handful of instances where he was challenged, and how he managed to be successful in the end. He sure is a great mentor and guide.

I liked that the author used his own life experiences in demonstrating how one is a natural leader. He reflected on his own life and upbringing and observed how his parent's parenting of him contributed to him being a successful leader in the aspects of life he found himself in; be it as a son, father, husband, or a doctor. This made the notion of one being naturally born with leadership qualities more believable and relatable. I liked the most that the author provided a self-assessment tool for readers to evaluate their potential leadership and become victorious leaders in the roles they found themselves.

There is nothing I disliked about reading the book. The structure of the book was perfectly set - each chapter focused on a category of leadership qualities and how the reader could harness them. The table of content made it easy for one to navigate through to the qualities they were interested in without having to read the entire book to locate them. I immensely enjoyed reading this book, and it covered a wide range of topics I found to be interesting, such as clinical intuition and observational skills. My vocabulary greatly benefited from reading this book, and my understanding of what it means to be a leader grew profoundly.

I, therefore, **rate the book 4 out of 4 stars**. There were no grammatical errors found in the book, pointing to the fact that it received professional editing. The book structure made the book easy to read, and the flow of the book was smooth. I believe that the book can be relied upon in identifying and developing one's leadership qualities since it received numerous awards, including The Pacific Book Award, meaning it can be highly recommended. I recommend the book to anyone who wants to become a successful leader and wants guidance on how to become one.

******

2018 Book Award

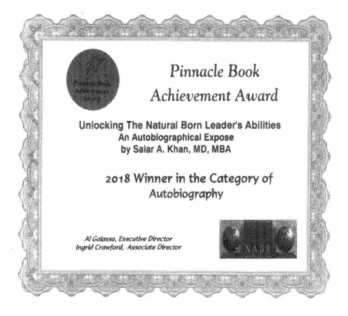

1. Pinnacle Book Achievement Award 2018 Winner in the Category of Autobiography by NABE (The National Association of Book Entrepreneurs).
2. The Pacific Book Review -Selected "TOP 5 Reviews for June 2018."
3. Book entered for annual book contest "Pacific Book Awards for the 2018" category of Autobiography as 5th Annual Pacific Book Awards FINALIST 2018 under Category "Best Memoir"

PACIFIC BOOK AWARDS

2018 FINALIST – BEST MEMOIR

Unlocking the Natural Born Leader's Abilities

Written by: Salar A. Khan, MD., MBA

Awarded by Pacific Book Awards on May 20th, 2018

CEO/President

E. Adams
Editor in Chief

Book Reviews

Review Date January 4, 2018   Reviewed by: Allison Walker

It is said leaders are not born, they are made, but according to Salar Khan, MD., MBA. some people are natural-born leaders. Everyone is born with hidden qualities to discover, some of which make people into natural leaders, Khan writes in his book, "Unlocking the Natural Born Leader's Abilities: An Autobiographical Expose." Leadership is a behavior, but it is also a mindset, Khan firmly believes. Until you discover how to unlock and foster that mindset, your success as a leader is limited. "Unlocking the Natural-Born Leader's Abilities" aims to help budding leaders discover and foster the leadership mindset. Throughout, Khan uses his own experiences to demonstrate how the leadership qualities he lists helped him succeed in his career and, most importantly, in his life. The book is primarily autobiographical. Although Khan makes an excellent effort, especially in the latter half of the book, to guide readers through the necessary qualities of a natural leader. This book is an easy read and offers great suggestions to achieve success in today's society both on a personal level and professional level.

Khan is quite a likable and engaging narrator. He masterfully weaves his own life lessons and leadership skills in his personal story for others to benefit from. You get the distinct impression Khan truly wants to help people, and his history serving as a mentor and guide to young people supports this. In the latter half of his book, Khan's advise for would-be leaders grows strong. He lists the qualities he found most helpful in the many supervisory roles he served throughout his career, and properly relates stories to extrapolate on each quality. Khan takes the time to create a few helpful flowcharts and a self-assessment tool, a throwback to his time spent as a college professor. The checklist pulls together the scheme of the book, and asks readers to think critically about their own successes and failures as leaders.

Don't be afraid of failure, Khan advises. Among the qualities of a natural-born leader are self-confidence and intrinsic motivation; natural-born leaders are driven to succeed, and by not considering failure an option, do not fear it. Instead of fearing failure, have the self-confidence to expect and strive for success, he writes. Khan's own eventful, international life is leadership by example, and exactly the kind of guidance his reader's need to unlock their own innate leadership qualities. If you're ready to make a change in your life, this book is full of valuable information and resources to support you along the way. I would highly recommend this book to professionals with a desire to leave a mark on the world, and a need of some guidance about how to do so effectively.

Review Date November 27, 2017   Reviewed by Donna Ford

"…natural-born leaders…have an innate skill set conducive to becoming leaders. They are optimistic, selfless, and do not seek external rewards or glory."

Illustrating the author's own journey to leadership, this autobiography/ memoir was written to pass on experience gained by a lifetime of service. A young child at the time of the India/Pakistan partition, his family resettled in Pakistan. With those early years in turmoil, his parents were his teachers. Once the author entered school, his brilliant older brother became a role model. Challenged by his family, the author assumed responsibility for household duties and volunteered for additional tasks. On his father's advice, Khan became a doctor serving in Pakistan, Saudi Arabia, and America. From experience gained, he declares it our duty to find out what we are capable of.

As if reading the short and prophetic wisdom of King Solomon, we discover the traits Khan considers significant to Natural Born Leaders (NBLs). They do not fear decision-making because they are not afraid of failure. They seek great success. They desire to motivate others because of concern for future generations. They must communicate confidently. The author defines self-confidence as informed intuition. This skill is of special value to any professional, especially a doctor.

Anecdotes in the book demonstrate how Khan's clinical intuition grew via residency and hospital work. Frequently, he diagnosed a mysterious illness by recognizing body presentations. A hajj pilgrim was in the medical ward with the distinctive posture of tetanus but with no visible entry point of infection. It occurred to this doctor that the man might have hemorrhoids—which was the case. A decision maker, a role model, and productive person, Khan's personal goal is always 100%. This 110-page, indexed book challenges readers to strive toward similar goals. The author also provides a self-assessment tool to help the reader determine if he/she already has, or can develop, the necessary gifts to be an NBL.

RECOMMENDED by the US Review

Review Date June 15, 2017

In Unlocking the Natural Born Leader's Ability: An Autobiographical Exposé, Dr. Salar A. Khan shares wisdom he has gleaned through decades of experience as an internist and pulmonologist in three different countries: Pakistan, Saudi Arabia and the U.S. Throughout, he weaves together autobiographical elements that illuminate how he became a leader with guidance on how readers can develop their own innate leadership abilities.

Khan divides leadership abilities into two categories: convergent thinking and divergent thinking. "Convergent-thinking leaders," he writes, "have a limited predetermined number of options and will look for data that supports one or the other." Because of this, they miss choices that could, in fact, be superior to those being considered. Divergent thinkers have a greater capacity, notes Khan, to "deal with stressful situations honestly, confidently, and intuitively and are creative, knowledgeable, charismatic and sociable."

Khan stresses the importance of developing your intuition, insightfulness and self-confidence and includes the following as key leadership characteristics: integrity, the ability to communicate effectively, sacrifice, patience and composure, open-mindedness, courage, compassion, and optimism. He believes that the pursuit of internal happiness is better than the pursuit of money.

Khan writes in an engaging style, and anecdotes of his own journey prove compelling. He reveals how six of the 11 children in his birth family died between the ages of two and four because of "global health issues." Stories of his upbringing in Pakistan, meanwhile, show intriguing ways that supportive parents can positively shape their children's future. Khan also shares detailed anecdotes from his medical work that illustrate how he developed his own natural born leadership tendencies.

Also, available in hardcover and eBook.

Review Date May 31, 2017

What are the book's strong points that make the book stand-out among other books in its specific genre? The book has essentially relatable possibilities to all audiences and not necessarily specific to a certain group/market/interest. This is a brave attempt to share perspectives in a form of fiction rather than the cliché of stating general occurrences. A highly readable book that deserves a wide range audience. This book was written as if the author had years of practice in making the implausible plausible since this is a superbly realized portrayal of the possible future.

What would most likely contribute to the book's success? At this point, the book is not known to the general audience and it needs consistent marketing and exposure through the help of decision makers and their connections

Preface

Where has the time gone? I am sixty-two years of age now, and the world is changing at a dazzling pace. I was thinking about writing this book over the last few years and decided to write it after retirement, until an incident made me realize how unpredictable life can really be. On Sunday, March 6, 2016, at about 6:00 p.m., the thirty-six-year-old son of my elder sister was sitting on a carpet at home, working on his laptop. My sister was sipping some tea in the same room as the news droned on from the TV. It was a typical lazy Sunday evening. He had no history of any illness when, suddenly, he dropped dead on the carpet. There was nothing—no warning, no signs, and no symptoms. In two to three seconds, he had already departed. Life honestly doesn't play on anyone's timetable except its own. And so I was compelled to start writing this book in December 2016.

This autobiography is written to illustrate my journey to leadership and to provide readers with a tool to evaluate their potential leadership qualities and become successful leaders in any organization—political or nonpolitical, corporate, nonprofit, government, executives, managers, health-care sectors, and so forth. I feel that these qualities are imperative to combating the adversity that leaders face and to showing how they can take corrective action to move forward from these situations. Leaders exemplifying these qualities are what I dub *natural-born leaders* because they have an innate skill set conducive to becoming leaders. They are optimistic, selfless, and do not seek external rewards or glory. Instead, they seek a sense of internal satisfaction and happiness.

By natural-born leader (NBL), I do not wish to open the argument between nature vs. nurture. Everyone has the natural ability to lead, in my opinion, but it needs to be harnessed and developed. An NBL is someone who has succeeded in this endeavor. Leadership, as will be demonstrated in the book, is to take action in line with one's principles and to inspire people toward a common goal. These two features are something that everyone should be capable of. Some might argue that everyone can't reach this state, but you will never know if you do not try. There are many instances in my life where I chose to take a chance, and those moments helped me realize my potential. Personally, becoming a doctor was definitely one of those choices. I was absolutely set on becoming an engineer, but in my final year of high school after my father floated the idea, my interest piqued, and the rest was history. This is to say that courage and a certain boldness are needed in order to be an NBL. It is not easy, but accepting the many trials and tribulations of life gives us an opportunity to uncover our hidden talents and skill sets. Life lacks charm without challenges, and those challenges show us who we are and offer a glimpse of what we can become.

In my opinion, individuals who receive intensive training to become leaders are not very confident in their own abilities; they are hesitant in their decision-making, encapsulate a fear of failure, and consequently are less successful in their endeavors. This is because they obtain training to try to develop leadership skills or even go it alone. On the other hand, natural-born leaders are target-oriented, fully focused, self-confident, and intrinsically motivated to accomplish their tasks. These leaders enter a certain uninterruptible state of flow when working on their task because they are fully absorbed in their work, not paying attention to any factors external to that task. Once they return from this state, they feel a sense of pleasure that invigorates them, allowing them to use their unique skill set to tackle further projects.

This autobiography will provide a further understanding of who these leaders are through personal anecdotes in hopes of providing guidance to those who are seeking to become leaders. This book is as much an exploration of leadership as it is an autobiography. I implemented various principles and applied them through the various projects I performed while living in Pakistan, Saudi Arabia, and the USA. Furthermore, I have outlined a performance-based tool that takes into account many of the qualities essential to natural-born leaders. The tool utilizes an easy scoring system that will assist one in determining his or her leadership abilities. By using this tool, people can discover if they have the abilities to determine if they can become powerful leaders in their respective organizations.

The idea for this book came from trying to understand how I came to where I am today. I went through many hardships and challenges in this life like everybody else. I learned many lessons, which allowed me to become successful. We all live on this planet for such a short time. What does it mean to live a life that is fulfilling? It often means that we have to take charge and responsibility in life—in essence, to be a leader. Today, I am a research compliance officer at the Jesse Brown VA Medical Center in Chicago. Over my time on this planet, I have played many roles: son, student, tutor, doctor, chief of medicine, acting director of medical services, acting hospital director, acting director for a nonprofit, acting administrative officer, father, and husband. This is a story of my experiences. And it is my hope that perhaps some of the things I have learned can be of use to you, the reader.

Due to the many roles I have played and the successes that I have had, naturally I became curious about the basis of leadership. Much has been said about attaining leadership skills, such as having the proper charisma, proper training, and other intangibles. Personally, I think leadership is a mind-set, and through my writing, I hope to convince you and help you realize that you too can achieve it. I think leadership boils down to being able to take action that is in line with one's principles and what's important to you.

Introduction

Have you ever wondered what it took to be a natural-born leader? What it means to be successful? Success always leaves a trail and this work portrays my fifty years' worth of experiences and observations. In this time, I've played many roles from physician to medical college professor to healthcare executive to family man. With lessons embedded throughout the book and a self-assessment tool at the end, this book will set the blueprint to your success. Leadership is a habit we cultivate. Life isn't easy, but that's part of its charm. It throws many trials and tribulations our way to help us rediscover who we are. In doing so, we become stronger, more capable and in the process can help make the world a better place. Learn from my experience: read each word, follow my lead, and do not hesitate to act. Only then can you awaken the natural-born leader within.

Leaders orchestrate commands to people in order to accomplish pertinent objectives and in accordance with their personal principles and intentions. This book sets to identify the qualities and abilities of a certain kind of leader, which I refer to as the *natural-born leader* (NBL). The NBL possesses innate traits that are refined and perfected over time with education, training, and experience. I will attempt to illustrate these traits by drawing from my fifty years of personal experiences, and I hope readers will look at this as an opportunity to introspect. I have also designed a self-assessment tool so you may self-evaluate the presence of these NBL abilities and identify where you ultimately fall on the spectrum. Today, there is a widespread lack of confidence in leadership—whether in business, government, education, or elsewhere. The vision of a confident leader—that of an NBL—is needed for the betterment of the world.

This book is relevant to any leader who is part of an organization. Whether they are students, medical residents, fellows, attending physicians, medical directors, hospital directors, or profit or nonprofit organization executives, they will find various examples in my journey from ordinary person to a natural-born leader (NBL). The goal of my book is to teach other people how to think and make decisions that work through observation so that they can achieve their dreams. Take a lesson from me, and apply it. The scope of this book is to find out if you have hidden NBL qualities.

The NBL looks at problems in many different ways. I believe that curiosity is an expression of a human being's motivation to wonder about the world's mysteries, to study everyday problems, and to find promising solutions. The NBL has this desire to explore the unknown, which leads to discovery. As human beings, we are tasked with discovering these solutions by investigating the unknown. The solutions are out there; we just have to discover them rather than invent them from scratch. Curiosity is a quality of NBLs that is related to inquisitive thinking by exploring, learning, and investigating our surroundings. This is evident in humans and other animals alike. Successful people seem to have basic personality and character traits that lead them to great wealth and accomplishments. Some of them use one combination of skills to achieve their goals while others use a different combination entirely. Despite these differences, all of them have the same basic skills that they use. To know what these skills are is to know your own chance of becoming successful. This is my take on what those skills are.

If one has a clear vision, a skill set to implement an action plan, intrinsic motivation, no fear of failure, self-confidence, and the ability to set a daily self-target, then one will achieve *flow* in accomplishing one's goals. Flow is the state in which challenges and skills are equally matched, playing an extremely important role in the workplace, defined by the Hungarian psychologist Csikszentmihalyi. Because flow is associated with achievement, its development could have concrete implications in increasing workplace satisfaction and accomplishment. Flow leads to an optimal experience, which means attaining a state of being hyperfocused and having effortless control, full alertness, and peaking of one's abilities. Only then will you feel real internal happiness that will make you refreshed and relaxed, bolstering self-confidence in your own abilities and a readiness to tackle new projects. If you maintain flow, it will lead to becoming an NBL. If anyone has these abilities, I believe they can change this world.

Everyone seeks happiness. Power, money, beauty, and health will not lead to happiness on their own merit. These alone can't lead to happiness. Although it sounds clichéd, ask yourself whether these things can truly lead to your happiness. The meaning you seek lies within you, and nothing in this whole world can give it to you. Many people are already afflicted with anxiety and boredom. The following is my recipe for happiness. Since childhood, I never ran after money or these external things in order to show the world that I had arrived, that I mattered, and that I existed. I am happy with what I have and satisfied because I find meaning in my struggles to live according to my principles.

My mother used to tell me to work with sincerity and not fret over wealth; if it was in my fortunes, I would receive it. I learned that how we approach life is important. In my own life, I worked in Saudi Arabia as a physician and hospital director until I moved to the United States and started at ground zero. Even though I had accomplished a lot, the only job offer I received was for a grocery store on Devon Street in the West Rogers Park neighborhood in Chicago at below minimum wage. Later my luck changed, and I got a job as a baggage scanner at O'Hare Airport for five dollars an hour. Many in my family back in Pakistan questioned my decision. We lived in a cramped apartment and without a car; the first Chicago winter was difficult. Through it all I never questioned my decision. Life was hard. Often, I would wonder if things were going to work out. However, I knew I made the decision for the sake of my family. If I had only cared about money and was married to my lifestyle and not my principles, then it is hard for me to imagine the kind of person

I would be now. I was a doctor working on minimum wage. Things improved afterward when I got my MBA and later started working as a research compliance director. My mother's words have continued to ring true, and from this I hope you can see that your relationship with money should not dictate who you are as a person. There is no harm in earning a lot of money if you can, but remember it must be earned in an honest way to avoid guilt, which will follow you your whole life. It will lead to anxiety, depression, and unable to sleep without pills. You have gained high status in society and own millions of dollars but have no internal happiness. If you are not happy despite a lot of money, what is the use of this money? You cannot buy happiness with money. Always try to focus on your internal satisfaction to have a happy and joyful life.

This begs the question: How does one develop this mind-set? Don't focus on the negativity in life, and if anyone is having a dispute or difference of opinion, then address it. Own up to your mistakes, if any, and move on. If the mistake lies in the other, then it is better to forgive instead of being consumed by righteous indignation, because we are all human beings and, by nature, imperfect. Everyone has been created in this world with a few strengths and many weaknesses. If I think of myself in other people's shoes, I will forgive them because I realize that I too am also full of weaknesses. While I am not proud of my numerous weaknesses, I do not look down on others, and I go immediately to my important work without distraction. This leads to more productivity for organization where I work, and I tackle bigger projects to enhance the reputation of the organization. The same mind-set can also help in serving humanity to the best of my abilities. For leaders, it is important not to take revenge but to instead learn to control their emotions, avoid burnouts, and try to maintain peaceful environments. The NBLs are honest and balanced in their decisions. There should be no personal ego involved in decision-making.

These are my personal experiences, and this is my journey to becoming an NBL. I hope many readers will look at this as an opportunity to reflect and to discover if they have NBL qualities based on a self-assessment tool I have generated at the end of this book. If you identify missing features, then it can give you areas to work on. It is an ongoing process.

How do you do the right thing at the right time? You do it by applying the values that are important to you. It is our duty to find out what we are capable of. My book will give you an idea to find yourself and your abilities to utilize hidden leadership qualities for the betterment of this world. Today, there is a widespread lack of confidence in leadership, business, government, education, and elsewhere. Every leader needs to regain self-confidence and maintain trust.

Chapter 1

Family Background

Who am I, and where did I come from? My parents migrated from India to Pakistan in 1947, immediately after India obtained independence from the United Kingdom (Great Britain) as two separate nations: India and Pakistan. My parents lived in Allahabad, Uttar Pradesh, India. The frequent Hindu-Muslim communal riots forced my parents and thousands of others to migrate from India to the newly created country of Pakistan. I was born on July 1, 1954, in Karachi, Pakistan, and was raised therein. I had a total of eleven brothers and sisters, and I was the eighth born. Unfortunately, six of my siblings passed away by the age of four due to global health issues at the time. Things did not get easier. In 1965, an Indian airplane came to attack and bombed Karachi. All of our family and neighbors hid in the trench in the open area behind my house. These were incredibly frightening moments in my life.

I was homeschooled in math and English for three to four months prior to obtaining admission to the fifth grade after passing an entrance exam at the Karachi Boys Secondary School in Nazimabad. I was always among the top of my class, which I attribute to my older brother, who served as my role model. He was a genius who was renowned throughout the school for his intelligence. I always had to work really hard to understand topics. My efforts eventually paid off as I passed tenth grade with the highest marks in math, chemistry, and physics. At a young age, I knew I had a gift for observation and a photogenic memory. I was also highly disciplined and obedient. My parents played a large role in establishing the environment that led to my success.

I was always attached to my parents. In fact, they were my first role models as leaders. My mother was a very gentle individual who managed all aspects of the home. Due to the kindness in her heart, she used to feed the poor in our neighborhood. My father was the chief superintendent of the Telephone and Telegraph Department in Karachi.

In the ninth grade, my classes changed to begin in the afternoon. As a result, I would complete my schoolwork the night before, and come morning, I would be bored as I waited for my classes to begin. However, this was a blessing in disguise because I soon realized that by having the mornings to myself, I could spend time with my mother. So one morning, I asked my mother if I could help her. I helped her in the kitchen and with cleaning at home. My mom was incredible. There were six of us in the family, and to prepare fresh food three times daily—efficiently and with incredible taste—in addition to doing other household tasks such as laundry and cleaning, was no small feat.

The thing I noticed most was that her time management was impeccable. My siblings and I had to go to school at slightly different times within a ten- to fifteen-minute margin. My mom worked within this time frame to make breakfast, such as scrambled eggs, roti (homemade bread), and tea, in unique ways to meet our personal taste preferences. And the process would repeat for lunch and dinner with other dishes such as lentil soup, chicken curry, and rice. She was truly the queen of the house. By helping her, I learned how to accomplish things in a limited time window and with deadlines in mind.

She prepared a variety of foods without any recipes, using ingredients without any scaled measurements. I can still taste her food on my tongue today. By observing her cook throughout this portion of my childhood, I can now prepare more than one hundred types of Indian and Pakistani foods with my own recipes, for up to one hundred fifty to two hundred people alone.

The way I built self-confidence was just by doing it. Doubt didn't exist for me because I had seen my mother do it countless times. The first time was on summer vacation in 1972, and luckily, no one was at home. I ended up burning everything. I cleaned everything up and tried again later. It is important to never shy away from being a beginner. Every failure taught me to understand the real composition of salt and spices that go into a delicious meal. I always taste the salt and spices in the beginning and commit to memory the chemical composition to ensure future accuracy of taste. With trial and error, I always aim to improve.

My father also played an important role with his high expectations. If I was among the top three students in my class, he would motivate me to reach the topmost rank. He would review my graded tests and exams with me, showing me where my shortcomings were. He would also give the example of my brother and why there was no reason I couldn't reach that level as well. This only spurred me forward. I never felt defeated or felt that the goal was too high to reach, mainly because I saw a way forward—a way I could improve and have little doubt in my ability. To this day, every obstacle I face motivates me to achieve the full outcome of any project, because I know I can.

My father knew his kids' natures very well. He noticed that my elder brother was a genius in mathematics, and he became an electrical engineer. He went on to become the chief electrical and mechanical engineer at Aga Khan Medical College University and Hospital in Karachi, where he worked for several years. I was also outstanding in mathematics like my brother, but my father noticed that I was always willing to help anybody in our neighborhood who was sick or needed aid. He also knew that I excelled in my studies, so he wanted me to become a doctor. I trusted my father's judgment. I had been preparing for an engineering career, so I changed tracks. My self-confidence did not waver. Still, it was difficult studying premedical subjects, including biology. Back then, biology also included zoology and botany. On top of that, there was only one medical college in Karachi—Dow Medical College—and it had only

4

forty-nine seats for open merit. It was a do-or-die situation. I accepted the challenge from my father, promising to do my best.

I did not realize how much self-confidence I had even at that time. This was perhaps due to the seemingly insurmountable success already achieved by my older brother, who was in his second year of engineering college. My rank in class was identical to my brother, so my self-confidence soared. If my brother could do it, why couldn't I? I just had a vision that I could do it. I was very confident due to my previous success at school, my ability to cook delicious food, my similarity to my older brother, and the reassurance from my parents. So I strongly believed that nothing was impossible and that anyone had the ability to make the impossible possible by working extremely hard without burning out.

I was studying at least fifteen hours per day, including college class time. My study room was on the second floor. It had no door or windows but had a roof made of iron sheets as a temporary arrangement. I remember the rooms were very hot in the summer and very cold in the winter when I studied there from 1970 to 1972. I never complained about the weather because it was a challenge. The challenge didn't deter me. I never felt defeated by the largeness of the wall that loomed above me. Every fall energized me to get back up again. I did not feel the harshness of the weather or the volume of studying I needed to do. My sole focus was to find ways to push past these obstacles. This was a state of flow as described by Hungarian psychologist Csikszentmihalyi. After taking my exam, the waiting game began.

In 1972, a neighbor came to visit and asked if I could help a young man he knew at a bank. That person wanted to pursue advanced training in business, but he needed to pass the general coursework. He had already failed the chemistry class five times, and that was his last chance. Otherwise, he would not be able to pursue any further education, per board of education policy. I agreed to meet him. I still remember his long face when we met at his house; he had no hope to pass the exam in the eight days. I was not a psychiatrist or psychologist at eighteen years of age, but I wanted to help him accomplish his dreams.

That boy had no hope of passing the exam due to his fear of failure. I was self-confident, and I made immediate eye contact with the depressed boy, who was twenty-one years old. I smiled. I told him it wasn't a big deal. I did that to show him that the challenge was not as insurmountable as it appeared. I really wanted to help him through it. My neighbor trusted me to help this boy, and I did not want to betray his trust. After we introduced ourselves, I talked to him for thirty minutes, assuring him that he would pass the exam if he followed my instructions.

I had seven days to teach him chemistry and to help prepare him for his exam. It was simple because, fortunately, I excelled in chemistry and remembered the vast majority of the information. I prepared studying material for him by writing eight questions that would mimic the types of questions he would encounter on the actual exam. Through moral support, assurance, proper guidance, and spending three to four hours daily on explaining the subject and having him write down what he learned at the end of each session, he began to understand chemistry. There were days that he could not meet me at my house, so I would reassure him by walking thirty minutes over to his place.

I also appreciated his resilience and helped build his confidence, which worked very well for him during the next few days. Then came exam day, and he answered six out of the seven exam questions, in which six questions needed to be answered. After finishing his exam, he was beaming with optimism and delight. He complimented my way of teaching as well as the positive vibes he got from me. He passed with a high score, and his overall grade vastly improved. That student told me that now he could continue his business education and thanked me profusely. My neighbor stated that it was only possible due to my charismatic personality, hard work, and honesty. I accepted that challenge as a volunteer to devote my time and effort leading to success.

As a leader, it is important to learn how to motivate. Motivating a depressed individual is not easy, but people need to follow and must be willing to be led to where we want to take them. Also, being able to be sincere in our dealings with other people is crucial. It was not so much my doing but rather my faith that I could help him and faith that he had what it took to pass. I didn't write him off. I would explain concepts to him at a rudimentary level before explaining them at a more sophisticated level.

Thinking back, our family placed a premium on education, and so much so that many of the neighborhood kids would come to be tutored at our house. I remember that our relatives used to drop off their high school kids at our home for six months to two years to get an education and training from my older brother and me. Our parents provided free accommodation and food to them. Now those kids have good positions in highly reputable organizations, and some have become engineers. Those kids got intrinsic motivation from our home environment and now are successful in their careers.

After a couple months, I got my own medical school entrance exam results, placing me among the top ten in the whole city of Karachi, and I easily got admission in Dow Medical College to fulfill my dream. I remember that that was the happiest day of my life for my father and me. After becoming a doctor, I felt that I was born to be a doctor; and I provided free treatment to all my neighbors and relatives and quickly built a reputation in my neighborhood. I drew out my talent to evaluate patients' diseases and quickly reached a diagnosis with my strong observation powers. As a leader, it is important to persevere and, I would argue, to have principles that are important to you and the self-confidence to tackle any challenge that comes your way.

I remember that my father was working as chief superintendent at Telephone and Telegraph (T&T) Department in Karachi, Pakistan. He was a hardworking and principled individual as well. He also sacrificed many things in order to help his children succeed. For example, he received an offer to work and visit West Germany for six months of training in telephone and telegraph technology in 1967–68, but my father refused and recommended someone else from his office for this training because, according to my father, he did not want his kids to get distracted by his out-of-country training visit, which might affect our education—particularly for my older brother, who was in his first year at Nadirshah Edulgi Dinshaw (NED) Engineering College. My father sacrificed for our future, which paid off later on in the form of having accomplished professionals at home. My father's way of life was imprinted in me.

I considered my father as the epitome of a hardworking, principled individual. He always had the forethought to prioritize long-term goals over short-term ones, such as getting promotions, benefits, or increased salary. He made well-informed decisions and sacrificed his career for us. I also followed in my father's footsteps by leaving my job as an internist and pulmonologist in Saudi Arabia and Pakistan and coming to the United States for the sake of my two sons. Now, I am able to see the fruits of my sacrifice as both of my sons are studying in medical school.

I also learned risk management from watching my mother cook as she altered various food ingredients to develop new flavors in the food at big parties at the potential expense of the eaters not enjoying the newly prepared dishes. In my career, I have taken several risks, and on rare occasions, I have not succeeded. In those latter circumstances, I immediately analyzed my failures and moved on to the next level of success. Having a photogenic memory also helped when making risky decisions.

In Lucknow, India, in 1983, I remember they served a special dish called *mutanjan* at a marriage reception. In 2014, this dish from thirty-one years ago suddenly came to my mind—the colorful rice, mutton meat, and various dry nuts. Since then, we have scheduled a party of forty-five people at home, serving mutanjan along with other dishes. My wife was afraid that no one would like it. Still, I was curious to know what would happen. And so I prepared it. I imagined the ingredients and kept adding ingredients, trying to re-create the taste from 1983 without a recipe. Nuts, pepper, ginger, cardamom, sugar, and salt were all thrown into a dizzying combination to make this sweet but salty and spicy dish. On the day of the party, many asked what it was, to which I said, "Eat it, then I'll tell you." Cooking food is as much an experience as it is a connection to the past. So for me, I wanted to connect the feelings I had for the fine dining experience and share it with everybody else. They were not disappointed and asked for the recipe. This high-risk endeavor resulted in a high-reward outcome. I suppose, in 1977, my father saw right through me when he proclaimed I would become a good chef.

Parents' Role in My Leadership Development

In looking back on my career and accomplishments, I believe I would not be the person I am today if it weren't for my parents. My father would come home after working a long day to sit down and practice mathematics and English with me from 1964 to 1969. So thank you for showing me what hard work looks like, for showing me that nothing comes easy, and for showing me that countless hours of hard work really do pay off.

I would also like to thank my mother for teaching me how to become a respectable, professional, and well-rounded individual.

Whether I was helping her with cooking or cleaning, I thank my mother for making me realize that I'm worth everything in this world.

My parents gave me the strength to stand up for myself and expect nothing less than the very the best, showing me true love in its rarest form, what it feels like, and how it can extend beyond life's obstacles and challenges.

My parents taught me to have a clear goal before starting an activity and to have the self-confidence to complete a task. This leads to success, producing a feeling of internal pleasure and happiness.

I can teach you through my early childhood as I learned from my parents. Goals entail circuitous paths that begin with achieving control over the contents of our consciousness. Our perceptions about our lives are the outcome of many forces that shape experience, whether positive or negative. Most of the forces that affect us are out of our control. It requires dedication, motivation, and hard work to be focused on accomplishing a goal. Elusive goals cannot be attained by a direct route. Every parent must spend time with kids in order to give them the self-confidence to tackle life's hardships since this will always lead to success in life.

My mother was often telling real stories, telling those with moral values verbally so we could keep our undivided interest and enjoy listening. She would tell us stories about the monkeys that used to frequent the house of my grandfather, who was the head of the police department in Varanasi (its old name was Banaras), Uttar Pradesh, India. She described how they would take care of people and how they would make extra portions for the local monkeys. The virtue of being of help to others served as the seeds to my own moral compass leading to my leadership qualities.

I continued this practice with my two sons for ten years almost daily between 1994 and 2003. The following article is published in

"The Waiting Room Magazine," by the International Association of Health Care Professionals (IAHCP).

Healthy Parenting—Storytelling: Path to Healthy Kids

Storytelling can be a vehicle for parents to bond with their children, while at the same time instill timeless, moral values and cherished character traits. It is often said that the quality of time spent is better than the quantity of time spent; making a ten-minute story a great way to directly connect to our children in the fast-paced world we live in.

Storytelling has been a tradition as old as human history. The stories of Aesop come to mind. The goals have often been to teach a moral lesson and to pass on wisdom. In some ways, it is a dialogue carried from the past and echoed into the future.

I want to ask you to take this dialogue a step further. Rather than simply repeating traditions and folklore of old, tell a story that relates to you in some way. In other words, relate something that is personally meaningful, and so when you tell the story to your kids, they can sense your own enthusiasm and connection. This was the exact formula that I followed when I would tell stories to my kids when they were young. My inspiration came from my own childhood, stories that my mother told, and my own personal experiences.

I would spin stories about a grandmother dealing with mischievous monkeys of many different colors and with many different traits. These monkeys worked together, setting aside their differences and toward a common goal. Often for a mischievous purpose, perhaps for which the grandmother would scold them; still they learned to accept each other and become better monkeys. My children would listen, hanging on to every word and every action of these characters that came to life in their imagination. Even when my eyes would be tired and my mind drained, I could always count on my youngest son to shake me and ask, "What happens next?" His eyes were brimming with excitement and enthusiasm that could hardly be contained in his small frame. Often, it was the only motivation I needed to continue.

Children are imbued with curiosity and are often the gateway to critical thinking. A story explores distant worlds and connects with characters different—yet somehow similar to us—all painted language. These stories are also not without benefit. Research by Dr. Lee et al. has shown that telling classic stories such as George Washington and the Cherry Tree could instill in children good moral practices like telling the truth. As parents, our job is to nurture these traits. However, we are often at the mercy of so much to do with very little time available.

Now that my kids are grown up, I can say that my kids have definitely instilled moral values such as compassion, honesty, and courage, which have the power of advancing children's minds. Now the question is, what stories should we tell and how should we narrate them? In my experience, they don't have to be complicated. If you can design a story from your own experiences or even a modified story you heard while growing up is sufficient. The most important thing is to be able to have fun.

Parents should tell these stories on regular basis at bedtime as a way to at least until they are ten years of age. Although a story can be found and read at the click of a button on the Internet, the social and bonding experience of telling a story to one's kids in person is irreplaceable.

Story time was a very special time for me and my sons because it was fun. It can help your child develop listening skills and get your undivided attention—a rarity in today's day and age. As long as the storyteller is willing to weave stories, a child will always be ready to hear the simplest of them, traversing unforeseen destinations that only the imagination can capture."

References: Lee, Kang. "Can Classic Moral Stories Promote Honesty in Children?" *Psychological Science*, 13 June 2014. Web. 26 Nov. 2015

Readers can also implement these principles in their lives to be good role models for their kids by personally coming up with creative, imaginative stories and verbally narrating them to their children instead of reading stories from a book. This ingenuity in the storytelling process will keep kids interested and bolster their creativity as you come up with the plot as you go. My two sons derived much benefit from this form of storytelling. They excelled in their respective classes, and now both are attending medical school. I am always thinking about the future generation, and from time to time, I am giving my neighbors' and relatives' kids advice. It is my belief that if all parents implement these principles, our kids will be more focused and become creative thinkers.

Chapter 2

Teaching of Natural-Born Leader (NBL) Abilities, Traits

Human beings are created with many unique abilities. They are created with the element of curiosity to discover new knowledge in order to create progress in this world. All newborns know how to breastfeed by nature and do not require any education. Similarly, ducklings know how to swim, and again require no education. Based on these two examples, I am sure we have millions of people in this world with hidden talents and skill sets which need to be identified at initial stages of life in order to realize their NBL abilities as it was done by my parents when I was a child.

In my opinion, there are various stages to life, and these stages have new experiences and observations that help us develop our NBL abilities, which are already hidden in our genes. Below I will try to go over the techniques and behaviors that were instrumental for my development.

Parents play a key role on a daily basis to spend time with their kids to provide the foundation to build self-confidence by reassurance, which is necessary to make a difference on this planet.

Phase 1: Infant to Childhood (Ages 1–11)

Children are vibrant and have unlimited amount of energy. Similarly, when I was in this age group, I had full freedom to play all the time since I didn't start school until the fifth grade. My mind was fully relaxed; that helped me think, explore, and learn without fear of making mistakes. I think in some ways this helped me build the confidence I needed, which has paid off to this day. My father homeschooled until the fifth grade, teaching me how to read and do math, which fostered a strong bond between us. This may not be practical in today's world, but I want to point out that placing children in an educational system focused on grades and constantly meeting evolving standards places a lot of pressure on them to perform. So what can a parent do? The basic idea is that parents need to be involved in their children's lives. As far back as I can remember, my parents had always been involved in my life from an early age to guide, challenge, and encourage me. The following are some suggestions:

> Strengthen the thinking process by telling verbal moral, thoughtful, humorous story at night for ten minutes prior to sleep. When I was younger, my mother used to weave many fantastical stories out of thin air for her kids. As a child, it was a wonderful ride. And as a parent, a story provides an opportunity to bond with your child, improve moral values, and help you spend quality time with him or her. Children can sense your own enthusiasm. This was the exact formula that I followed when I would tell stories to my kids when they were young. My inspiration came from my own childhood, stories that my mother told, and my own firsthand experiences. For example, I used to tell my children a story about mischievous monkeys that would pull pranks on an elderly lady, eventually learning to be kinder to her. They would listen attentively. Storytelling is very insightful to kids as they develop their imagination and sharpen their memories by engaging themselves in these stories. It will only develop once the kids find themselves interested in good, moral, thoughtful stories. I have my example of telling stories to my two kids daily for ten years. As an NBL, imagination is key to seeing opportunity around every corner. Also in the busy world we live in, finding ways to connect with our children is priceless.

My father used to test my math and verbal skills on a daily basis. I also did the same for my children. For example, my youngest son would always perk up when I would give him basic addition, subtraction, and multiplication questions. This helps kids build confidence in their thought process and reasoning ability in a low-pressure environment where grades and constant judgment are not the norm.

I remembered I used to go with my father for grocery shopping to a store that was twenty minutes walking distance from my home. My father would ask me to pay attention to our surroundings during the walk to the market, telling me he would help me build a photogenic memory. At this age, it was a fun challenge for me, and I would put my heart and soul into looking at objects with care so that I could meet my father's expectations. When we came back home, I remember that he asked about one beautiful new house during our walk. I answered light blue, and my father would nod approvingly. In this way, I learned to increase my observation and sharpened my memory of my surroundings.

Helping my mother at home with laundry and cooking helped me develop my time management and organization skills, which have been the foundation to my career. By spending time with my mother, I noticed that I became more loyal, dutiful, hardworking, task-oriented, firm, direct, opinionated, and to the point. The more confidence I built and the better I performed, allowed my parents to involve me in home decision-making. Their sincere appreciation and respect for my efforts left an impression on me. I built a self-confidence and understanding that I can be more assertive in decision-making. In this way, I gained inner control, inner calm, and greater awareness that I could accomplish what I set out to do. As parents, we need to instill the environment for kids to develop these traits. My parents gave me freedom to do things, make mistakes, and work independently. I would be scolded if I did things incorrectly, but overall my parents were very supportive in showing me the right way to do things.

The impact of these practices led to the gradual development of my NBL abilities. My thought process was fully charged moving toward positive thinking, and toward building strength and eliminating weakness and negative thinking, which leads to laziness. These features gave me the power of intrinsic motivation to accomplish my daily tasks at home and school. In this way, I felt more energy and power to do extra work with a high level of competency due to strengthening my thinking. I started helping old people in my neighborhood buy groceries, bring medicine from the pharmacy, and take them to the nearby hospital for follow-up. By doing this, my feelings toward suffering people became very strong. This led to a question by my father in 1970: "I wish to have a doctor at our home. Could you fulfill this desire?" My confidence in my abilities and my desire to help people coalesced into a profession that encompassed all of this, so how could the answer be anything other than a resounding yes? In this way, I believe our actions and the confidence behind them lead us to our ultimate destiny.

Phase 2: Adolescence to Midlife Fifties (Ages 12-49)

During ages *twelve to nineteen*, I became ready to accept more challenges and developed love with myself and people around me to help anyone who was in trouble as a part of life. My passion and my emotion were very strong, and I was ready to do something extraordinary to satisfy my internal happiness.

During ages *twenty to thirty-five*, I developed a strong courage and enterprise to perform job excellence. I took on more responsibilities and gained more confidence in my NBL abilities.

If at this stage your childhood has not gone perfectly, then make small targets and find ways to accomplish them. It was only by doing that that I was able to learn what I was capable of. And as I did more and fell more, I began to improve and develop confidence. At the end of the day, through the successes and failures, your belief in yourself to accomplish and to do something meaningful should never falter. No matter how small the success, be able to appreciate it as a step along the journey. No matter how great the failure, be able to see it as a learning opportunity.

In midlife ages *thirty-six to fifty*, I started focusing more and more on clinical and leadership intuition, which enhanced my decision-making abilities leading to NBL. At this age individual reach a certain threshold of strength, and dominance begins to assert and playing prominent role in the organization. My multiple experiences in life helped me build an intuition of how to get things done as efficiently as possible. This phase for me was about taking more responsibilities and getting a better understanding of what I can do.

Phase 3: Mature Adulthood Ages Fifty Onward (Ages 50-Onwards)

In this phase, people need to develop compassion and kindness to establish in their work life and become contributors to the betterment of society through mentorships and other forms of philanthropy. This has led to great internal satisfaction for my accomplishments.

However, it is important to keep learning and remain self-motivated to continue to improve. We must combat complacency. It is important for people to seek opportunities to polish themselves and to lead to a mark in this world. Place yourself into the shoes of others to understand any kind of human sufferings. Have self-confidence, self-motivation, and clarity of vision. Be goal-oriented, honest, and sincere with others. Always be ready to sacrifice for the greater good and not for greed and money. Money comes and goes, so it is not a great indicator for success. True success comes from chiseling the heart with morals, virtues, and discipline to finally become a person of worth. See the following infographic to see how the journey looks like. What will your legacy be?

Cultivation Process of the Natural-Born Leader's Abilities

Following this path should cultivate these 10 qualities:

1. **Insightfulness and self-confidence.**
2. **Intrinsic motivation**
3. **Integrity-unlocking trust**
4. **Communication**
5. **Sacrifice**
6. **Patience and composure**
7. **Open-mindedness**
8. **Courage**
9. **Compassion**
10. **Optimism**

New problem with sincere desire to solve it and become NBL.

Use personal base knowledge of issues and informed perspectives to find the root cause

Approach with a positive attitude and think outside the box.

"Always remember the solution is out there when we have a sincere desire to resolve the issue"

Focus on 2-3 definite solutions, judge according to currently available data.

"Be ready for positive or negative outcome to handle situation using quick adaptation to control situation"

Continuing these processes repeatedly, the mind learns "out of box thinking", quickly responding to complex challenges

Intuition builds insightfulness and vice versa (see ch. 4, 6 and 7)

"After a few cycles of repetition, you will realize your hidden capacity and skill sets"

Self-confidence develops faith in one's abilities.

Cultivate sharp vision => Clarity of goal => Easier to plan and execute actions

Leads to positive outcome with success

Cultivation of intrinsic motivation- a path to pleasure and happiness

Leads to hyperfocus and next level of "State of Flow"

Gain optimal experience and find hidden talent and skill sets

Internal pleasure and happiness

Chapter 3

Could I be a Natural-Born Leader?

Everyone is born equal

There is no universal definition of leadership. It can come in different flavors. It boils down to making decisions and taking actions according to an individual leader's principles. It depends upon the thinking style of the leader and his or her advisers. This book is about being a natural-born leader and giving ideas to readers about other kinds of leaders. But the world needs the best kind of leaders, who are NBL, in my experience and observation, otherwise the future of leadership is dark because we do not have an established program on how to bring out hidden talents and skill sets starting from childhood and continuing for a lifetime. It is an ongoing process starting from the home environment and the quality-care neighbor environment, and then the environment at schools, colleges, universities, and the environment at various organizations and institutions on which our career depends. I can tell you how we can start with building a foundation for everyone. The home environment starts with parents' nature and personality. Maybe they are not loving or respecting each other, have an abusive nature, or show anger and fight all the time. The first thing parents will need to do is understand each other, try to compromise for the sack of newborn, and start practicing creating a calm home environment for the newborn; otherwise parents will be responsible for destroying the life of the newborn in the future. In this way we may lose valuable human beings and create trouble making people. First, start from home. It will be a long journey but will be very effective in the near future. Parents themselves must learn about discipline, respect, love, and proper organizational skills at home by doing domestic work to create a learning environment for the upcoming kids.

I can define NBL according to my experience and observation that each human being is created with many unique abilities. They are created with the element of curiosity to discover new knowledge and find hidden talents and skill sets that are already built into our genes; we must unlock these abilities by accepting additional tasks and challenges at work and in life to see if we are capable of doing them or not. If we found positive results of these activities, it means we have abilities to convert impossible to possible, which enhances our self-confidence, keeping alive intrinsic motivation, and becoming more target oriented, which brings you internal happiness. Now you can claim you have NBL abilities to handle any situation with a positive outcome in order to create progress in this world. The NBL has the ability to provide groundbreaking ideas, which lead to the career of world leaders. The NBL is superior to acquired leaders, who got trained through various workplace training but are not confident and are afraid of failure or losing a job. The NBL's ability to hyperfocus gives effortless control on a situation with self-confidence to lead.

My journey to evaluate my own personality started during my childhood through my parents and continues even today. I went through various hardships and many ups and downs in my life. At each step, I learned how to bring out my own personality, and I had a knack for immediately correcting myself to further refine my abilities.

I believe that every human being is created equal and each one of them possesses the essential qualities and abilities of an NBL; it is simply a matter of bringing hidden talents and skill sets to the surface. According to my personal observation, experience based on trial and error, application of strong self-analysis of my mistakes and corrections on a daily basis, and finally my education helped to develop intuition as a doctor and as a leader during my last fifty years, starting from the age of twelve.

I unlocked at least my several hidden capabilities and converted them into abilities to perform under adverse situations with strong positive outcomes due to self-confidence, self-motivation, no fear of failure, strong faith on my own abilities, clarity of vision and goal, and know-how to get results. Now my mind is tuned to think out of the box to find unique solutions to issues. Now I realize that all these abilities were built in as an NBL, which I unlocked during my life and work career, and which make me feel that I am highly internally satisfied, the happiest man on earth. I strongly believe that there are hundreds and thousands of people around the globe leading people with confidence due to their perfection of work in whatever field they are working. Human beings are created with the element of curiosity to discover new knowledge in order to progress in this world. If they are lacking a few abilities of NBL, they can learn from my book.

In my estimation, human beings were created with many hidden qualities and characteristics, which they start using in their lifetime even without any education. I grew up in a developing country where most people are illiterate. Nonetheless, I still knew many high-functioning individuals with no formal training who were running great businesses. This came to show me that there was something natural about leadership that could not be taught in a classroom but was rather cultivated from within. When one thinks of a leader, the first thing that comes to mind is a political leader or any successful CEO or entrepreneur; some of them may very well be NBL.

I have a strong belief that the progress in this world is made because of the uncanny abilities of these natural-born leaders. The NBLs are always firm in their decision-making due to the confidence in their own abilities and their vision of the future in successfully accomplishing short-term and long-term goals.

In my career, I found myself working under time-sensitive, high-risk, and high-pressure situations, which allowed me to unlock and develop my natural-born leader (NBL) qualities. Therefore, my present is very much a product of everything I have done throughout my life. As a child, I had always taken responsibility for all household chores, developing my time-management and organizational skills. Obedient and disciplined, I was ready to help everyone even though I would be very busy in my studies. I would always find time to help others, and being there for them gave me a sense of internal satisfaction. After becoming a doctor, I would without hesitation treat patients in my neighborhood without expecting anything in return. My parents were always modeling a clear set of virtues and qualities such as respect, honesty, arduous work, self-sacrifices, discipline, and determination. As I gained more confidence in my abilities, it would set the stage for my successes as an internist and a pulmonologist, and as a chief of medicine, as an acting director of medical services, and an acting hospital director in Saudi Arabia under the Ministry of Health (MOH) without any additional salary. I could do this because I never considered my occupation as a *job*, but I treated it as a calling. I was working toward a vision for the sake of the hospital management and patients to serve humanity to create a better world. I always set targets for myself in advance as they relate to my job, home, and family needs. Completing my tasks such as achieving deadlines, I tell my heart that I have completed this task, giving me happiness and igniting my desire to start the next task of the day. This type of feeling will not come automatically; you must be intrinsically motivated to achieve this state. You have to break your day down into tiny bits that are manageable. Even things as simple as taking the trash out, cleaning your room, and really anything else can be a source of joy and fulfillment. These abilities made me more target-oriented, focused, self-confident, and intrinsically motivated to accomplish tasks.

As an NBL, I developed a cohort of abilities and qualities over time that make me a great role model and help lead others. Today I am self-directed and often establish norms. I have developed the ability to inspire and motivate others to accomplish their goals with positive outcomes.

As an NBL, I have an intuition, which is difficult to describe, but, personally, I think it entails having an art of observation, and integrating nonverbal information during high-risk, time-sensitive situations. I have obtained clinical and nonclinical intuition through my career using this approach, and I have been able to make several crucial decisions. Strong leaders are the ones that the company and other employees can trust because of their values, integrity, and morals.

Maintaining clear and consistent communication with everyone is also something I cultivate every day. Constant communication makes employees understand the company's vision, giving them an assurance that they are working toward the desired goals. Confidence is essential for strong leadership when the future of their company, corporation, or organization is at stake.

Furthermore, I have possessed clinical intuition through my work as a physician, and a nonclinical intuition through my experience as a director of research compliance and administrator. This pair of intuitions has allowed me to make decisions in novel circumstances— those in which I have no prior experience. As I have noticed in my career on so many occasions, I am very good in finding immediate solutions for complex issues, yielding strong, positive outcomes. My experiences have built my intuition, allowing me to have epiphanies when searching for solutions. To me, it feels as natural as breathing.

In daily life and work, these are the most important characteristics that must be cultivated as an NBL. Later in the book the reader can find detail, with examples to have a better understanding of NBL abilities to perform as a strong, confident leader.

1. Insightfulness and self-confidence. Insightfulness is the deep understanding of task or challenge, which reinforces intuition in a continuous cycle and results in well-informed decision-making and positive outcomes. When observing the fruits of decision-making, it will serve to build self-confidence. It leads to developing clinical and leadership intuitions.

2. Intrinsic motivation. This is the desire to accomplish tasks or do activities based on internal rewards for one's own pleasure and happiness.

3. Integrity-unlocking trust. This is the most difficult concept to teach leaders. It depends upon honesty and the moral and ethical values of individuals, which develops the trust of the public in their leader or patients in their doctor.

4. Communication. This is the art of conveying information between two or more parties. It starts with listening to others and observation skills required to recognize the nonverbal message to come up with appropriate responses. It is a part of the patient-doctor relationship. Successful communication with patients develops trust, and patients will become more open. This is the art of taking good history from patients about illness. Leaders communicate with the public or CEOs communicate with staff to operate work with flow.

5. Sacrifice. The biggest part of my success is accepting challenges and doing additional projects without expecting any rewards. The people who are doing the job are usually not flexible and are reluctant to take on additional projects to work, but throughout my career I was taking additional projects and making sacrifices to my personal time for my internal happiness. This attitude led to my hidden talents and skill sets and more exposure to adversities to gain confidence.

6. Patience and composure. This entails having the ability to tolerate, withstand, or avoid certain frustrating actions or behaviors. This is important for leaders and doctors.

7. Open-mindedness. This is the ability to accept novel ideas and thoughts into one's repository of thoughts. It means thinking outside of the box considering unique uncommon solutions to common and uncommon problems we face on a daily basis.
8. Courage. This is a quality or mental state that allows one to face difficult challenges and overcome fears with confidence. Leaders and doctors have courage to make tough decisions when necessary.
9. Compassion. This is an ability to motivate people, to listen, to maintain eye contact and to show genuine concern. As a doctor, it is also important to let patients know that you are interested in treating and trying to reduce patient suffering or as a leader in addressing the genuine concerns of the public with sincerity to assure the public that as a leader you are ready to sacrifice for them.
10. Optimism. This means to think about positive outcomes being as equally possible as negative outcomes. Always have positive thinking to convert a negative outcome into a positive outcome.

NBL Desire Built inside the Heart, Not as a Learned Trait

Prior to working in Saudi Arabia, I did not have what I call leadership intuition because I never got the chance to play a leadership role. It was tough in my early tenure working in Saudi Arabia because the hospital director wanted me to accept the position of the chief of medicine. He praised my insightfulness, self-confidence, and composure in the medical field. I give him immense credit due to the intense pressure and scrutiny he placed me under, giving me the opportunity to see what I was made of. I think finding out who you are, where your values are, and what you are capable of are all integral to becoming an NBL. I think everyone has these things built into them, and the challenges life throws at us help us unlock them.

Those struggles led to my first leadership position as the chief of medicine, which ultimately served as the stepping stone in developing my leadership intuition. This included integrity, communication, open-mindedness, insightfulness, self-confidence, and composure. These qualities provided me with the foundation to manage about two hundred hospital staff, doctors, and nurses, and to treat approximately sixty-five thousand patients in outpatient, inpatient, ICU, and ER services in Saudi Arabia from 1988 to 1993. I was working eighteen hours a day and having one day off every two weeks. This allowed me to combat complex issues in a timely manner even until today.

I unlocked my hidden talents and skill sets in Saudi Arabia as internist and pulmonologist, and soon the hospital director promoted me to chief of medicine, later acting director of medical services and acting hospital director. This was from 1988 to 1993. I unlocked my NBL abilities in this span, which I was only vaguely aware of before this span. As I found myself rising to the challenges and finding success, that further led to building my foundation as a self-confident leader with clear vision about my goals and about full implementation.

Employees Dissatisfied with Managers or Bosses

Today, leaders (managers) strive to be truly understanding of others and have a desire to build a strong culture but are often burned out due to the concomitant stresses of leading their respective organizations. I believe these leaders lack the proper mind-set to overcome these hurdles. The skills to work with our minds and our emotions and with other people are essential but rarely developed. According to Gallup 2013, leaders failed to provide genuine leadership to *70 percent of employees who were disengaged and had low productivity and innovation.* Only 8 percent of people strongly agree that they experience overall well-being because of their work.

In my observation, leadership is a combination of talents and hidden skills. Research on leadership indicates that 50 to 75 percent of organizations are currently managed by managers who lack leadership competence. Many leadership researchers have weighed in on NBL, but, surprisingly, there is very little literature that fully explores this theory.

Managerial leadership can come in different flavors. One way to think about it is according to the differences in thinking styles, namely convergent and divergent thinking. Convergent-thinking leaders have a limited predetermined number of options and will look for data that supports one or the other. They don't consider things outside the box and, consequently, miss answers that can be equally viable or perhaps even superior. Divergent thinker leaders always think out of the box and find various solutions for the same issue and can make clear, strong decisions with confidence and with positive outcomes. This is the quality of NBL. I have my thirty-seven years' experience to use my clinical intuition as a doctor, and leadership intuition as a chief executive officer (CEO) taught me how to reach on-balance decisions according to the available information based on my previous observations and experiences.

Many leaders, therefore, just end up following the status quo, unable to lead due to fear of failure. They are unable to take risks; they play safe and don't address issues until they spiral out of control. These leaders do not trust their own abilities. When leaders become followers of the status quo, they make excuses and blame others for deficient performance. Therefore, employees are mostly dissatisfied with their mangers or leaders.

Changing Trend of Leadership Role

According to my personal observation during the last two to three decades, the majority of leaders developed a fear of failure and of losing their jobs, which led to reduce confidence in their own abilities and job securities. Therefore, leaders want to play safe to keep their jobs, and they become more defensive. Now most leaders are scared to take change initiatives in the institutions or organizations, which is the main cause of suffering and shutting down the organization. This leads to a vicious cycle of low morale and low trust in their own abilities, which further leads to poor productivity and decreased expectations. Failure of leadership further erodes trust in management. Failed leaders are quitting jobs and are redeployed in other organizations, and if failure continues then they are removed from a company. If they luckily succeed, then they play defensively to maintain their position. Now time is money, life is fast, the expectation of success of the organization is very high, nearly everyone is materialistic, market competition is tough, and it is difficult to find a job according to the skill of the individual. Job mismatch with skill is also a huge issue these days, which probably leads to burnout. Fear of failure is the major issue, due to which leaders developed reduce focus on issues, which leads to reduced clarity of mind and losing control; therefore, leaders are not accepting challenges or not taking any chances due to a lack of confidence. Many leaders choose to follow instead of to lead due to fear of failure, and, unable to take risks, they play safe and keep quiet when thing get worse. These leaders do not trust their own abilities. When leaders become followers, they make excuses and blame others for deficient performance.

During my childhood, life was simple because I grew up in a third world country; people were not too materialistic, they were sincere, there was a lack of social class distinction among people, and the markets were not very competitive. Leaders were comparatively confident and had the skill to run the organization.

Difference in the NBL Abilities:
International and National Level

There is no difference, in my observation, between NBLs internationally and nationally. This is because they are all intrinsically motivated and, in my opinion, are less materialistic in their personal lives. There is a sense that they never use shortcuts in life, are authentic, always put sincere effort into performing any task, and most of the time accept challenges with full dedication. They always went through a self-process of deep observation, thinking, analyzing their own personalities, correcting negative thinking (I called it weakness), and always approached life positively.

I think, however, the environment affects how leadership evolves. For example, in the United States there is a perception of stakes being much higher for failure than there is internationally. In places such as Pakistan, with poverty being so widespread, there may be less of a social stigma attached to failing. For example, if a person becomes a baker after failing to gain entrance to medical school, there is less stigma due to the difficulty of becoming a professional in a country such as Pakistan. In the United States due to stigma, it may lead to more of a deflection of responsibility. For example, in the aftermath of the BP oil spill in 2010, one of the executives famously remarked that "they would like their life back" and "what … did we do to deserve this?" To be clear, leaders such as these are present both nationally and internationally. The NBL way is to take responsibility, analyze what went wrong, and rise to the challenges to contribute to something larger than self.

I believe the world is facing a crisis when it comes to leadership; our society needs more positive thinkers. We need the vision of a confident leader—that of an NBL is needed for the betterment of the world. This was my main motivation and inspiration for writing this book. My observations and experiences throughout the last fifty years of my life also have served as an inspiration. I remembered that my parents provided a foundation for achieving self-confidence by teaching me to set smaller tasks or targets in my daily life. Having a clear goal in mind is imperative to achieving success—free to make self-decisions and analyzing mistakes, and after achieving a target or a goal, feeling happy and self-rewarding yourself.

Through this book, I want to generate a positive-thinker class of people, and true NBL in the world leads to the prosperity of mankind and reduces negative-thinker leaders or destructive types of leaders in order to avoid world crises in the form of wars and a lot of human suffering.

In my opinion, this world would be a better place to live depending upon our world leaders and which way they want to take this world. We are losing great talent before people come to play their constructive roles. Life is very short to do good things and to make new discoveries in every field for making a paradise on this world. Always try to do good things and help humanity and try to reduce human sufferings.

The scope of my book is to teach readers how they can find NBL capabilities and abilities based on my years of experience and observation. As I am strongly convinced that I am an NBL, why not you too?

Chapter 4

Education, Training, and Experience
Create Strong Observational Skill

A Foundation of Clinical and Leadership Intuition

Everyone is born equal with several hidden talents and skill sets to bring to the surface their NBL capabilities and abilities by being exposed to complicated projects and issues. There is no harm to try; you may be an NBL.

Leadership is a mind-set and a behavior. You should discover and unlock that mind-set to become a successful leader. This book aims to cultivate your NBL abilities and achieve success on a professional and personal level. The book has flowcharts and a self-assessment tool to find your hidden talents and skill sets to become an NBL. I experienced an eventful international life as a leader will provide the exact type of guidance the reader needs to unlock his or her own hidden leadership qualities. If the reader is ready to make a change in life, he or she needs to follow valuable information and resources to leave a mark on the world as an NBL. A decision maker, a role model, and a productive person, my personal goal is always 100 percent. I also provide a self-assessment tool to help the reader determine if he/she already has, or can develop, the necessary gifts to be an NBL. Natural-born leaders have an innate skill set conducive to becoming leaders. They are optimistic, selfless, and do not seek external rewards or glory. From experience gained, I declare it our duty to find out what we are capable of. Leaders do not fear decision-making because they are not afraid of failure. They seek great success. They desire to motivate others because of concern for future generations. They must communicate confidently. I define self-confidence as informed intuition. This skill is of special value to any professional, especially a doctor.

I divide leadership abilities into two categories: convergent thinking and divergent thinking. Convergent-thinking leaders have a limited predetermined number of options and will look for data that supports one or the other. Because of this, they miss choices that could, in fact, be superior to those being considered. Divergent thinkers have a greater capacity to deal with stressful situations honestly, confidently, and intuitively and are creative, knowledgeable, charismatic and sociable. I stress the importance of developing your intuition, insightfulness, and self-confidence and include the following as key leadership characteristics: integrity, the ability to communicate effectively, sacrifice, patience and composure, open-mindedness, courage, compassion, and optimism. I believe that the pursuit of internal happiness is better than the pursuit of money. This shows intriguing ways that supportive parents can positively shape their children's future. I share detailed anecdotes from my medical work and as a CEO that illustrate how I developed my own NBL tendencies. I had years of practice in making the implausible plausible, since this is a superbly realized portrayal of the possible future.

When I was obtaining my medical education in Pakistan, I had to go through a five-year program to receive my medical degree. The first two years consisted of basic medical science concepts pertaining to medicine, and then the next three years consisted of studying clinically related subjects to learn the diagnosis and appropriate treatment options for diseases. As a medical student, I remember being posted in various departments: general medicine; surgery; orthopedic surgery; ob-gyn; ear, nose, and throat;, ophthalmology; pediatrics; and psychiatry. I recall taking these clinical rotations very seriously, trying to learn the most I could from my professors and from the patients I observed. Our clinical patient education included long and short case presentations to the professor and head of the medical department.

Long cases entailed spending sixty minutes with complex patients to obtain a detailed history and full physical examination, and these cases were presented in front of the professor and other clinical group students. As a student, they served as a significant source of developing my early self-confidence because we were responsible for making the proper diagnoses and describing the treatment management of the patient. This served as the appropriate time to learn how to correct one's errors in diagnosis and to recognize the common clinical signs and symptoms that correspond to certain conditions. During this phase, the professor, who served as our preceptor, encouraged us to think outside the box when considering potential differential diagnoses and even consider the possibility of rare medical conditions. The long cases were the patients admitted for diagnosis and treatment for various medical disease conditions. It was our duty to follow up with the patients to evaluate lab reports and other diagnostics to clinch the correct diagnosis and treatment.

For the short cases, the senior doctor or professor allotted us students twenty minutes to examine patients with conspicuous clinical signs and symptoms. For instance, a patient would present with a heart murmur, so we would have to examine the cardiorespiratory system to check for cardiac and lung issues. Likewise, if a patient presented with a facial droop, we would have to conduct a neurological examination to determine if the patient was having a stroke. During these unique examinations, we were not allowed to speak with the patient or take any notes. In my three years of various rotations, I developed a solid foundation in my clinical intuition and to exhibit divergent thinking when considering solutions to the patients' medical issues.

My professor advised me to focus on the patient's clinical signs and symptoms, which provided "70 percent of the clue" in obtaining the appropriate diagnosis. In this way, we could minimize unnecessary lab work or imaging. This held especially true for poor countries such as Pakistan. With their limited resources, patients couldn't afford health expenses. Reconciling these conflicting issues allowed me to hone my clinical intuition not only to precisely ascertain diagnoses but to also understand the patients' perspective and their limited access to affordable medical services. Later in this book, I will provide you with several examples of how I developed this clinical intuition.

Today, the process of becoming a doctor is an arduous one with many hurdles and trials along the way. Generally speaking, medical students undergo a four-year educational program, and then proceed to become residents in specialties of interest, with some pursuing fellowships, and finally complete their coveted medical training, becoming full-fledged doctors. These new physicians can go many routes in practicing medicine. One route they can take is that of leadership, through which they can lead organizations and hospitals, join pharmaceutical companies, etc. The successful pursuit of these necessary routes entails learning as much as one can from each stage of his or her medical training and accompanying experiences. This allows doctors to develop self-confidence and enhance their out-of-the-box thinking.

Leadership is all about making decisions with confidence. Working in various disciplines of medicine will develop clinical intuition and a sense of open-mindedness when making medical decisions, which I believe are two key constituents of a great physician. Once doctors start practicing with a strong clinical intuition under their belts, they will really start enjoying treating patients and developing faith in their own abilities while eliminating unnecessary testing. As a doctor, always try to enhance your observational skills to properly identify clinical diagnostic signs and avoid any unnecessary lab work and imaging.

As physicians, we take the Hippocratic oath or variations of it in order to serve humanity. However, we often worry about the money and time invested in our chosen profession. Debt is a primary focus in the student's mind. Everything starts from the intention and the desire to pay it off. It will take time, but as your senior doctors paid off their medical education debts, the time will come when you will also be free of debts. By having this long-term vision and understanding, life will become more free-flowing and easier. I have also given this advice to both of my sons who are studying medicine. Money will automatically come from sources you couldn't once fathom. Don't compare yourself to others, since some are born into abundance and others have to work with great hardship. Make a habit to apply your knowledge and abilities to consolidate your new skill sets into practice, which leads to great success and your satisfaction.

As a leader, it is important to have an appreciation and understanding of as many perspectives and disciplines as possible. This is because, as a leader, you will encounter new territory and may not always know exactly what to do. Having as many tools in your toolbox as possible is therefore desirable. For medical students, I advise them to take each clinical rotation seriously and to not write a rotation off just because you don't think you will pursue it. Even surgeons need to have good history and physical exam skills as well as knowledge, even though most would consider it to be a very hands-on specialty. It is the time to learn the art of good history taking and systematic examination and spending time with patients to gain self-confidence and grasp clinical signs to more readily diagnose and treat future patients.

The same can be said to anybody else who expects to become a leader. You have a working knowledge of each part of your organization and how all these parts fit together. For a patient, if a doctor visits and advises a treatment plan and then goes away without any sympathy, only imparting vague get-well wishes, then no trust can be gained. Fear is the greatest enemy here. From a patient's perspective, everything seems to be breaking down, and they should have someone that can explain what's going on. For a leader, inspiring trust is very important.

I completed my residencies in general surgery, genitourinary surgery, internal medicine, and neurology in 1980–82. Here, well-informed and swift decision-making was vital. I started medical residency in general surgery, and after three months, I met Professor Dr. Syed Adib Hasan Rizvi, who worked in the urology unit at the Civil Hospital in Karachi, Pakistan, and who is now the founder and chairman of the Sind Institute of Urology and Transplantation (SIUT) at the hospital. Dr. Rizvi had offered me a one-year paid residency position in his genitourinary surgery department, assuring me that I would learn much in that short time and gain the self-confidence to manage patients and surgical procedures independently.

Throughout the course of this residency, I learned procedures such as peritoneal dialysis, hemodialysis, and urethral dilatation, and how to manage the critical patients under him. Surely, within that short span, the independence he gave me to tend to the urology patients boosted my self-confidence. These two factors in my early career proved to be the stepping-stones of my success in Pakistan, Saudi Arabia, and the United States.

After urology, I joined a six-month residency program in internal medicine under the late Dr. Professor Khawaja Moin Ahmed in Medical Unit II at the Civil Hospital in Karachi, Pakistan. I learned the treatment and management of various acute and chronic illnesses in internal medicine—rheumatoid arthritis, COPD, pulmonary hypertension, and lung, liver, and brain cancers, to name a few.

After this residency, I decided to work in the neurology unit under Professor Dr. Akhtar Ahmed for a six-month period, which helped me to diagnose and treat various neurological conditions, such as strokes, brain tumors, Alzheimer's disease, meningitis, and polyneuropathy.

After completing residency, I began working in family practice medicine for one year in Karachi, Pakistan, while continuing education to complete several advanced postgraduate certificate courses, which were equivalent to fellowships in medicine today. These courses included dermatology, cardiology, and advanced internal medicine at Jinnah Postgraduate Medical Center in Karachi, Pakistan. Later, I took an advanced course in tuberculosis and chest diseases at the Ojah Institute of Chest Diseases at the University of Karachi, Pakistan, for a one-year period in 1982–83. Having taken these advanced courses qualified me to take an exam for a degree in the Membership of College Physicians and Surgeons (MCPS) in Karachi, Pakistan, in tuberculosis and chest diseases in March 1985.

Author's Clinical Intuition Examples in Pakistan, 1985–1987

After completing my residency programs and additional medical courses, I began practicing as an internist and pulmonologist at the Karachi Psychiatry Hospital in Nazimabad, Karachi, Pakistan, from November 1985 to December 1987, where my job was to exclude medical illnesses from psychiatric patients getting treatment in that hospital—which, of course, necessitated an understanding of psychiatry. During that experience, I learned the art of distinguishing medical illnesses from psychiatric illnesses and had the privilege of diagnosing and treating both as an internist. For example, I witnessed patients who were treated for major depression and anxiety disorders; but through my evaluation, I recognized that they also had pituitary adenoma, thyroid tumors, and adrenal gland tumors. Therefore, I was able to identify the root cause of their psychiatric conditions, broadening my understanding of the role medical illnesses play in manifesting psychiatric illnesses.

Practicing at that hospital served as a big game changer in my life. I learned much about psychiatric illnesses, including anxiety disorders, panic attacks, mood disorders, depression, psychosis, schizophrenia, bipolar disorders, various types of epilepsy, and drug abuses. Along with acquiring a thorough understanding of these conditions, I learned the accompanying diagnostic therapies for them, including relaxation therapy, behavioral therapy, prescription of antipsychotics, and marriage counseling.

One technique I practiced and came to appreciate was the electroconvulsive therapy (ECT). This is a very effective procedure that entailed conducting small amounts of electrical currents to the bitemporal regions of patients' brains for a few seconds with or without IV sedation. This would cause tonic-clonic seizures and short-term memory loss, providing relief to patients presenting with acute severe psychotic symptoms such as auditory/visual hallucinations and delusions. Patients would then be started on antipsychotic medications to treat their psychotic illnesses. I myself had the privilege of performing ECT more than 150 times to treat these illnesses.

In 1986 at the Karachi Psychiatry Hospital, I vividly recalled the receptionist giving me the medical record of an established patient at that hospital and sent that patient to my office. The patient came to my office door, saw me, then immediately went back to the reception desk and told the receptionist that he did not want to see that doctor. The receptionist told him that Dr. Salar was the best doctor in the clinic. The patient acquiesced and was brought back to my office. As soon as I saw him, I recognized him as my professor of chemistry when I had attended college years ago. I respectfully stood from my chair and shook his hand. Immediately, he requested that I ensure his confidentiality when it came to the fact that he was a psychiatric patient. As a physician and former student of his, I respected his decision and reassured him that I would maintain confidentiality. He was very pleased that one of his students went so far as to become a doctor. After having talked to him, he revealed that he had schizophrenia and was being treated for it. He had received several ECTs and antipsychotic treatment during the last ten years. A mental status exam showed that he was mentally stable.

It was my observation at that time that most patients treated with a combination of ECT (three to five treatments) and antipsychotic medications returned to their normal mental state and were able to go on with their lives with regular psychiatric follow-ups. Since then, he maintained a monthly follow-up cadence until December 1987, when I began my transition to Saudi Arabia.

Knowledge and experience in psychiatry are very helpful to me because, in my clinical practice, I have seen many psychosomatic patients who needed different lines of management compared to patients with medical illnesses. Learning to differentiate the treatment and management of medical and psychiatric illnesses bolstered my self-confidence and decision-making ability. I would like to thank Dr. Syed Mubin Akhtar, owner of Karachi Psychiatry Hospital, for this wonderful opportunity.

My medical journey was a long one, but getting experiences in various faculties of medicine and surgery broadened my experience and foundation of my clinical intuition, which I enjoyed a lot during my medical career. Ultimately, my patients were beneficiaries of my treatment, and I thought I did justice with my profession, treating over twenty-seven thousand patients in Pakistan from 1982 to 1987. Now I feel satisfied with my medical profession by primarily having served humanity instead of making money out of this noble profession. My two sons are studying in a medical school in the United States, and I hope they will continue my legacy.

Author's Clinical Intuition Examples in Saudi Arabia, 1988–1993

I was chief of medicine from July 1988 to March 1993, acting director of medical services from July 1990 to July 1992, and acting hospital director from June 1992 to March 1993.

In June 1987, while I was still working at the Karachi Psychiatry Hospital, I saw an advertisement in the local newspaper for medical specialty and subspecialty positions in different hospitals in Saudi Arabia under the Ministry of Health (MOH). I decided to apply for an internal medicine and pulmonology position at one of those hospitals because of the prestige of working under the MOH in Saudi Arabia. Out of roughly five thousand applicants for the various medical positions, only eighty-six doctors from various specialties were selected. I myself was fortunate enough to be called for an interview in October 1987, and the following month, I was ultimately selected for a position and appointed as an internist and pulmonologist at the Al-Midhnab General Hospital in Al-Qassim Province under the MOH in Saudi Arabia starting in January 1988.

After joining that hospital, I witnessed many difficulties in the transitioning process. I met with the hospital director, who held the highest position in the hospital. He welcomed me to the hospital, giving me a briefing of their expectations, responsibilities, patient population, and common diseases. The very next day, I began working in an internal medicine and chest clinic. I was welcomed by the staff members—nurses, assistants, and other attending physicians, but, to my surprise, they informed me that the hospital director was very manipulative and assertive. He would cut the salaries of various staff members and unreasonably discipline them for their mistakes. This type of behavior induced incessant fear in their hearts. He had zero tolerance for errors and faults on the part of the staff.

The hospital director was also the attending ob-gyn, so he had medical skills in addition to administrative ones. He would always challenge the medical treatment options I would suggest for my patients, thereby putting me under immense pressure and challenging my medical knowledge. For instance, I remember that it was my third day working in that hospital, and I was on call. I received a call from the ICU that a patient, a ninety-year-old male, had a cardiopulmonary arrest and was listed in critical condition. Immediately, I went to the ICU, where the resident and nurses were managing him. His attending was off duty, so I took charge and followed emergency treatment protocol to treat him. He had a complicated case of type 2 diabetes with gangrene on his foot, a recent stroke, and congestive heart failure. I spent the whole night with him, providing all possible treatments at the time to save his life. I had used a cardiac defibrillator, intubated him to provide him a steady flow of oxygen, and had given him medications to treat his hypotension.

At 5:30 a.m., the patient suddenly woke up and asked about his son. I called his son, who was supposed to be in the waiting area, but he was not there. Within five minutes, this patient had expired. I completed the death certificate and other documents and went back home. It was 7:00 a.m., and I had to go back to work to start my duty for the following day starting at 7:30 a.m. As soon as I checked in, I went to the male medical ward and saw the hospital director sitting at the nursing station waiting for me. I greeted everyone, including the hospital director, who instantly addressed me. "Dr. Salar, I received a complaint against you from the patient's son." I saw that he had the patient's chart in his hand. A little perturbed, I asked if there was any wrongdoing in my treatment of the late patient. He said that he did not find any wrongdoing, but the patient's son was complaining that I was just "standing around."

I recognized that emotions generally ran high during those situations—high because of the patient's death. However, for someone to imply that I had not done anything for the patient? Whenever I do anything, I always give it my full attention. On top of that, I had full confidence from my previous experience of dealing with many dying patients to know how to work calmly with my medical team during those critical life-and-death situations. Normally, there is pandemonium during those types of situations, where attending physicians are chaotically managing these patients while concomitantly giving unclear commands to nurses and residents. This occurs to the point that these nurses and residents start panicking and are unable to successfully carry out these orders. In contrast, I tried to be very calm in ordering medical treatment to be carried out by nurses while injecting intracardiac adrenaline. When no response was noted, I was performing cardiopulmonary resuscitation and applying the cardiac defibrillator to revive the patient. Residents and nurses were happy with my critical-patient management style, mentioning my capacity to maintain control of the situation.

I had absolute conviction in saving that patient's life and was not afraid of losing my job. I wanted to do the right thing in every situation. Conviction is my principle. My mentors in Pakistan were calm, so that was where my nature had come from.

I told the hospital director, "You are creating unnecessary trouble for me. Right now, I am resigning from my position, so please return my passport and arrange a plane ticket for me to go back home." He was surprised, but I had firm faith in my management. I knew what I did was right based on my training. I came to acknowledge the fact that the hospital director was trying to be manipulative and assert his power over me. He had a domineering presence in the hospital and, from what I had heard, would cut salaries for frivolous reasons such as being slightly late to work in order to maintain his control. After this incident, I left the nursing station and went to my clinic to see patients. He was so infuriated by what I had told him that for the next months, from January to June 1988, he would try to find mistakes in my medical practice to warrant firing me.

That was indeed a period of trial and tribulation for me. However, I remained self-confident and resolute in my medical abilities. When you act based on principle, you have no regrets no matter how things play out. That is why I am always at peace.

Two weeks after this incident, I admitted a seventeen-year-old boy suffering from pneumothorax of his right lung. Pneumothorax is a condition in which there is a leakage of air into the pleural space from the lung alveoli. Essentially, the lung collapses in this process similar to how a balloon deflates when it is punctured. The patient came from a village and was not attending school. I decided to manage this patient conservatively during a five-day period, in which I observed the patient and provided relief to any acute symptoms he would experience in this span. For example, I put him on oxygen during his first day due to his shortness of breath and IV fluids to combat his lack of appetite.

Toward the end of this five-day period, the hospital director was on my back to insert a chest tube to remove the air from his pleural space to allow for lung expansion. I wrote in the patient's chart about why a chest tube would not be necessary for this patient because his symptoms had subsided, and he did not have any corresponding critical symptoms such as fevers and infection indicative of respiratory distress, which would necessitate inserting a chest tube. Furthermore, I was also concerned that the process of adding the chest tube would make the patient more conducive to infection and fistula formation. Instead, after conservatively treating the patient, I repeated a chest x-ray and found a 40 percent improvement in his lung perfusion in addition to noting improvement in his clinical signs and symptoms, such as coughing and breathing.

On the fifth day, I was in the clinic. I received a call from the nurse that the hospital director wanted to place a chest tube and prepare a referral to the chief of surgery to insert the chest tube. I complied with his request and had the chief of surgery evaluate this patient, who wrote, "I fully agree with Dr. Salar's management of this patient." Over the next three to four days, the patient fully recovered and was in stable condition to be discharged. Therefore, my diagnosis of pneumothorax was correct because, otherwise, the patient would not have recovered by my conservative method. The hospital director did not speak a word to me.

Throughout my time at the hospital for the next six months, I would find myself constantly being tested. But I persevered because I trusted my clinical intuition and my patient-management skills, and had confidence in my decision-making. I firmly believed that the patient would recover without any invasive procedures. These first six months improved my ability to work under time-sensitive, high-pressure situations.

The hospital director was closely monitoring my patient's diagnoses and treatments through my charts in medical wards, ICU, and ER. It was April or May 1988 when he received a call from the director at Buraidah Mental Hospital, who requested to talk to Dr. Salar. The hospital director asked him, "Do you have a complaint against Dr. Salar? Please tell me."

The psychiatric hospital director told him, "I want to acknowledge and appreciate Dr. Salar's expertise in the field of psychiatry." I was working in the ER during the call, and the hospital director transferred the call to me.

The psychiatry hospital director was very happy and pleased with the psychiatry referrals I had sent to Buraidah Mental Hospital and told me, "Dr. Salar, your diagnosis and treatment plans for referrals are very detailed and perfect. Despite our expertise, we usually follow your instructions every time we get a referral from you. In fact, go ahead and write your diagnosis and sign your name. It's good enough to know that Dr. Salar referred this case."

Such praise doesn't come overnight. Due to my prior experience at the Karachi Psychiatric Hospital, I have always been committed to successfully identifying and differentiating psychiatric conditions from medical ones. As a result, during the last few months since I had joined Al-Midhnab General Hospital, I had referred at least twenty to twenty-five various psychiatric illness patients through the ER to the Buraidah Mental Hospital with a detailed patient history, mental status examination, diagnoses, and treatment and management plans.

There was another salient instance where the hospital director tried to manipulate and exert his dominance over me. I was in the ER, tending to a patient with a case of right-sided hemiplegia. I thought that it could be a result of a thromboembolic or cerebral hemorrhage in the internal capsule of the brain. Right away, I prepared an order for a CT scan of the brain at a nearby hospital because our hospital was not equipped with this facility. For all kinds of outside imaging orders and referrals, we needed the approval of the hospital director and the director of medical services. As soon as they both saw my CT order, they immediately paged me and instructed me to come to their office. I recall that they were both very angry because to them, I was getting unnecessary CT scans on all my patients. For me, it was frustrating. "You are both doctors! Is there a way to tell if this patient's stroke resulted from a brain bleed or blockage due to thrombus or embolus? Only when I have gotten the CT scan results will I start treatment. If you won't approve, I will write on file that you both refused to perform a CT scan and will be held responsible." They were ready to flip, but in the end, they acquiesced because they did not want to be held accountable by the MOH. The scan came back and identified the thrombus as the cause, for which I started treatment, and within six weeks, the patient started to show improvement. After a six-month rehabilitation period, the patient regained his power and strength to walk with a cane.

Once again, I felt that I persevered through that trial, holding on to my resoluteness and courage to make decisions that I felt were appropriate for my patients without caring or fearing that I would lose my job at the expense of these decisions.

Starting in July 1988, after all the instances, I noticed a stark and peculiar change in the hospital director's demeanor toward me. He started to smile at me more frequently and stopped interfering with my treatment and management plan for patients. I think what happened was that all that time, he was trying to find faults in me to control me, but in the end, he gained respect for me. This is because an individual who acts according to his or her virtues and goals is difficult to oppose since that person has no weaknesses. He is not swayed by public opinion, only a sense of what needs to be done. I have always been focused on doing what is best for my patients. If I had to deal with verbal abuse, then so be it.

In that month, one day, he called me into his office and told me he had made the decision to make me the chief of medicine. In the beginning, I refused. He was a very difficult man to work with, and the idea that he just wanted to control me and inflict a barrage of pressure on me made me wary to accept such a position. Then he put pressure on me to accept the position because, according to him, I was the best physician in this hospital, and he was very happy with my performance in treating and diagnosing patients. He was especially impressed with my ability to diagnose rare medical cases and the respect I had earned from my patients.

According to the MOH in Saudi Arabia, that position or any higher position is only reserved for Arabic-speaking doctors. Though I had learned to speak Arabic fluently in six months, it added to my initial hesitation. It was my first foreign work experience. Prior to that leadership role, I never had any experience and skill in dealing with medical staff, doctors, and nurses or managing an entire medical department with fifty beds in the medical unit.

As the chief of medicine, I was given the responsibility of delivering lectures and case presentations as a part of continued medical education to medical staff, nurses, and doctors. The Al-Midhnab General Hospital was equipped with 144 beds and with all the facilities to diagnose and treat patients, except CT scans. I managed patients suffering from cardiac, neurological, pulmonary, and psychiatric illnesses. In addition, by practicing medicine in Saudi Arabia, many patients came from rural and agricultural areas. As a consequence of that, I was able to treat and manage several hundred patients with Mediterranean fever (brucellosis), an endemic disease due to drinking unpasteurized milk; approximately 160 patients with scorpion stings; one patient with a fox bite; five patients with poisonous snake bites; and one patient with a case of complicated tetanus. Through my leadership, I reorganized and expanded the hospital's medical departments based on our patient population by establishing a diabetes clinic, a diabetic club, and a *brucella* clinic. I also developed new policies and procedures for the hospital when it came to patient treatment.

I also generated a new unit drug dose system because the prior system resulted in the expiration of many medications, as the hospital would overstock on drugs, which would often go unused. The system I developed took into account the more common medications and their dosages that were used for all patients in the hospital. I made a list of the quantity of the dosages and quantity of each drug the pharmacy had for use and instructed nurses to mark the medications that were required for use that day. These nurses would then send that report to the pharmacy so that they may restock the exact number and type of drugs that were used that day. There would be a separate list for each ward to ensure that any discrepancies in drug usage by the inpatient ward could be avoided. This essentially circumvented the issue of overstocking on drugs, effectively saving money for the Ministry of Health in the Al-Qassim Region. It was a model hospital in the region. Other area hospital management personnel came to learn from us.

During this time, in April 1989, my mother in Karachi informed me that she met someone who would be a great candidate for marriage. Her name was Rubina, and she was doing her medical residency at the time. I was not provided with a picture or opportunity to meet her beforehand. I had complete trust and faith in my mother's judgment and choice, and I decided to proceed with the engagement. To provide some context, at least at the time, arranged marriages were a norm in Pakistan for cultural reasons.

On December 22, 1989, I took paid time off from the MOH as a part of my annual vacation to get married. The marriage was scheduled on January 6, 1990, which also happened to be the first time I saw Rubina. I said, "Wow!" I was really impressed with my mother's choice for marriage. I was immediately attracted to her, and at least from what she tells me, she was also attracted to me. We had a wonderful wedding in Karachi, Pakistan; and we had the reception the following day, both with over four hundred attendees. In February 1990, I returned to Saudi Arabia to resume my work. My wife later obtained approval from the MOH to come to Saudi Arabia in March 1990 to work as an ob-gyn resident at the Al-Midhnab General Hospital. We went on to have our first son, Faraz Khan, in December 1990, and our second son, Saad Khan, in February 1994 in Karachi, Pakistan.

The hospital director appointed me to the position of acting director of medical services in July 1990 due to my exemplary job performance. I prepared a major disaster plan against the biological and chemical warfare in the Gulf from August 2, 1990, to February 28, 1991. I launched a major disaster plan to cope with this warfare.

I also carried the responsibility of the chairman of various committees in the hospital, including the SUE (standardization, utilization, and ethics), quality assurance, law and regulation, brain death, and drug and pharmacy committees.

In August 1992, the MOH appointed me as the acting hospital director, which was the highest position in the hospital due to the official transfer of the previous hospital director to a different hospital. At that point in time, I held all three honorary positions: chief of medicine, acting director of medical services, and acting hospital director, while holding my original position as an internist and pulmonologist. It was a great honor for a Pakistani to hold all these positions in Saudi Arabia under MOH as a non-Arabic national. As per MOH regulation, all top hospital positions are only for Saudi nationals or for those from Arabic-speaking nations.

I played a crucial role in collaborative decision-making and consensus building by improving clinical management with the Ministry of Health on national health issues. I was regularly reviewing the utilization of hospital resources and staff and provided quality management and budget development for the hospital. I also organized a regional clinical symposium on cardiopulmonary resuscitation (CPR) and provided training to the hospital's medical staff on first-aid treatment of traumatized patients who were victims of the chemical and biological warfare in 1990–91.

Additionally, I developed a standard of operating procedure (SOP), which fostered an interdepartmental relationship between general surgery, ob-gyn, internal medicine, and ER doctors. In this way, the ER doctor would diagnose incoming ER patients and screen them to be sent to general surgery, internal medicine, or ob-gyn. According to the experience of the ER doctor, he will decide who he will call for consultation—a physician, surgeon, or an ob-gyn. This ultimately optimized the process of screening patients for particular treatments and avoided delay in patient consultation.

To illustrate the system before I established SOP, I recall a nineteen-year-old Saudi female patient who came to the ER with acute pain to the right lower abdomen for four hours.

Step 1: The ER doctor called the surgeon for evaluation to see the patient. The surgeon assessed the patient and concluded on the patient chart that it was "not a surgical case." Then, the surgeon recommended that the ER doctor call the ob-gyn to rule out ovary or uterine-related complications.

Step 2: The ob-gyn doctor did an assessment and concluded after examination that it was "not an OB-GYN case," instructing the ER doctor to call the attending internal medicine physician, who at the time was me.

Step 3: Next, the ER doctor called me to examine this patient, and after assessment, I diagnosed the patient with acute appendicitis. I called the surgeon to inform him that the patient was suffering from acute appendicitis, but the surgeon had already assessed the patient and concluded that she had no such case. During that entire consultation process, the patient was in limbo for two hours, waiting for treatment.

I decided to admit the patient in the medical ward with a diagnosis of acute appendicitis and recommended routine blood test and put her on nil per os (NPO), anticipating surgery and on IV fluids. The following morning, I began my rounds by visiting the patient first and asking the nurse about the patient's condition. She informed me that the surgeon took her to the operating room very early in the morning for surgery of acute appendicitis. After surgery, the surgeon apologized to me for not acknowledging my diagnosis of acute appendicitis sooner. The patient was ultimately treated by the general surgery service after her appendectomy and discharged a few days later.

The afternoon following the appendectomy, as the hospital director, I held an urgent, impromptu meeting between the ER, ob-gyn, and general surgery attending doctors to address what had transpired within the last twenty-four hours. After observing how that case of appendicitis was handled, I decided that we needed to optimize the process of operating on patients. The way the system worked until that point, as illustrated above, was that after a particular service had deemed that the patient did not need general surgery or an ob-gyn operation for females, the burden of responsibility would no longer be on their shoulders and would instead fall on the next service that was consulted. After careful discussion, we drafted a standard operating procedure (SOP).

The SOP worked as follows when a patient admitted to the ER was suspected of needing surgery or other critical evaluation:

> The ER doctor would call any attending on call (i.e., attending physician, surgeon, or ob-gyn), depending upon his or her judgment.
>
> Whichever of these three services called—let's say, for the sake of an example, surgery—would come to evaluate the patient and determine if surgery was necessary. If necessary, he would admit the patient under general surgery, operate on the patient, and thereafter manage that patient until discharge.
>
> If surgery was not required, the surgeon would be responsible for the final disposition of patient. Therefore, he would communicate with the internist or ob-gyn for consultation. In this way, they would work together as a team to decide what kind of treatment and management the patient would need instead of putting the responsibility solely on the service consulted. If both attending internal medicine and ob-gyn declared that it is not their case, then the surgeon would make the final decision on whether to admit the patient or provide treatment and discharge from the ER.

After approval of our signatures on the SOP, it was displayed in the ER to follow accordingly. The SOP established an interdepartmental relation and strong communication between these various services, and, in essence, avoided the repetition of similar incidences in the future. From the patient's perspective, it allowed for swift treatment and management of critical, improving patient care and satisfaction.

From Developing Intuition to Unlocking Leadership Abilities

By doing work in the medical field, I enhanced my clinical intuition. This helped me develop confidence and insightfulness in diagnosing and treating more than one hundred rare cases without any unnecessary testing. I would have a very clear plan of action in mind when tending to these patients. For example, in my clinical practice, I took a maximum of twenty to thirty minutes for evaluating new patients and ten to fifteen minutes for obtaining their medical history and physical exam. With this plan in mind, I was able to rule out several medical illnesses. Then I would consider any potential mental or psychiatric etiologies. I would conduct a mental status examination and finalize my clinical diagnoses by recommending selective lab work or imaging relevant to my clinical diagnosis. Otherwise, I would refer patients to other specialties with my final diagnosis and even with a potential treatment plan.

I remember that after referring twenty to twenty-five cases to a psychiatry hospital in Saudi Arabia, their hospital director called our hospital director to inquire about me and wanted to speak to me. He told me, "Dr. Salar, we highly appreciate your thoughtful and correct diagnosis and treatment plans for these patients, so much so that our psychiatrists rely on your diagnoses to treat these patients. They have become so relaxed! So next time, refer the patients with just their diagnosis and write your name." It was one of the greatest compliments I had received from a professional. It only happened due to developing a keen clinical intuition and having compassion for my patients.

As much as I enjoyed my professional work and success in Saudi Arabia, family concerns deterred me from renewing my contract with the MOH. On May 10, 1993, I visited my parents in Karachi, Pakistan, who were getting old and sick. In addition, my firstborn son, Faraz, was three years old at the time and was getting ready to attend preschool, so I wanted to ensure that he attended a reputable school in Karachi. Because of these reasons, I wanted to spend more time with my family. After discussing with them, I decided to finish my contract with the MOH on September 15, 1993, and return to Pakistan.

Suddenly, in August 1993, my father went into a heart attack. At the time, my older brother, who normally worked in Karachi, was on a business meeting in Islamabad, Pakistan, and one of my older sisters from the United States was visiting our parents. One of my nephews was engaged and preparing for his marriage, so three of my nephews, including the one getting married, were also out of the house. My sister wanted to spend time with our father, so she took him out for shopping one afternoon. Upon returning later that afternoon, my father started experiencing vomiting and chest pain. Suspecting a heart attack, my sister decided to take him to the closest hospital. There, they diagnosed him with extensive myocardial infarction and were unable to resuscitate him. He passed away later that evening.

I was very distraught at the time because not only did my father pass away while I was in Saudi Arabia, but I was also unable to visit him because my passport was with the MOH as they were finalizing the paperwork and documentation for the termination of my contract. It was also very frustrating because when I visited my father in May 1993, I took him for a cardiology consult because, as a physician, I suspected unstable angina. They performed an electrocardiogram [ECG or EKG] on him that showed normal sinuses and rhythm and other cardiac testing—all of which, at the time, were within normal limits. I nonetheless figured he still had some form of coronary artery disease.

This experience allowed me to understand and appreciate the importance and fragility of life. I want future doctors to be resilient and persevere if they are taking care of dying patients. In my clinical experience in Pakistan and in Saudi Arabia, about forty-five patients were in near-death situations, but after seven to eight hours of constantly working with these patients, some were brought back to life almost miraculously. One of these patients even had a straight line on the EKG monitor, indicative of no sinuses or rhythm. I started cardiopulmonary resuscitation by using a cardiac defibrillator two times along with other supportive treatment for ten to fifteen minutes. This patient's heart returned to baseline without any residual complications related to cardiac arrest.

To provide another example, I was treating a seventeen-year-old boy from 11:30 p.m. who was stung by a black scorpion and was in critical condition due to bleeding from all body orifices with hypotensive shock. I worked with this patient the whole night. And then at 6:00 a.m., his vital signs became stable, and he opened his eyes and began talking to me. At last, my hard work had prevailed. I persevered and thus succeeded.

Looking back at my time in Saudi Arabia, I highly appreciated the opportunity the hospital director provided me by allowing me to practice medicine at the Al-Midhnab General Hospital. In the beginning, he put me under intense pressure and scrutiny, which only allowed me to develop my intuition as a doctor. After pressuring me for six months, he promoted me to chief of medicine, opening a window of opportunity to take the clinical and nonclinical intuition I had acquired up until that point to uncover leadership abilities. These included integrity, communication, open-mindedness, insightfulness, self-confidence, and composure. These qualities provided me with the foundation to manage about two hundred hospital staff, doctors, and nurses, and treat approximately *sixty-five thousand patients* in outpatient, inpatient, ICU, and ER services in Saudi Arabia from 1988 to 1993.

Author's Clinical Intuition Examples in Pakistan, 1993–1994

In October 1993, after having just moved back to Karachi, Pakistan, from Saudi Arabia a month prior, I was looking for a job. I decided to visit Baqai Medical College and Hospital and inquire about any potential job postings. To do so, I needed to speak with the owner of the hospital, Dr. F. U. Baqai, who was also a renowned surgeon. However, it was unusually hard to get an appointment to meet him directly. I was thinking about how I could manage to meet with him. I paced back and forth in front of his office a few times, hoping his door would serendipitously pop open. Luckily, the receptionist noticed me and asked me if I wanted to meet the hospital owner. I said yes, and she told me that I would be next.

When my time came, she told me that I could go in. I entered his office and confidently told him about my experience in Saudi Arabia and presented him with my résumé and educational certificates and degrees. Dr. Baqai was very impressed with my educational and professional background and experiences. He immediately offered me the position of associate professor of medicine, but he told me to wait for a few days until the board of directors reviewed and approved my application. After three days, he called me to officially sign the contract.

With a desire to educate and serve, I gladly accepted the position of associate professor of medicine at the Baqai Medical College and Hospital in Karachi, Pakistan, which I served from November 30, 1993, to October 1, 1994. As the associate professor of medicine, I had the opportunity to continue seeing patients in internal medicine and pulmonology, while simultaneously getting the chance to teach medical and dental students. I was excited to move on to a new chapter of my life.

I would do my outdoor patient clinical from 9:00 a.m. to 2:00 p.m. and led lectures from 3:00 p.m. to 4:00 p.m. daily. I taught general medicine and subspecialty lung diseases to approximately one hundred medical students and approximately fifty dental students. During these lectures, I tried to engage with my students by being expressive. I would smile and move around the lecture hall, providing examples of pertinent patient cases from my medical experiences in Saudi Arabia to keep their interest in the subject high. I would occasionally tell relevant jokes during the lecture so that every student sitting in class could relax and laugh amid covering dense medical information. I also allotted two to three minutes each lecture to allow students to share their ideas and comments or to even share jokes to lighten the mood of the lecture. This encouraged free-flowing participation in the class and empowered them with the confidence to speak in front of a hundred-student lecture hall. On average, about 96 percent of students attended my class because of my ability to motivate and engage them to learn about medicine and pulmonary conditions.

I gave students the utmost respect and treated them equally during lectures. I would maintain eye contact with and approach them to assure they understood my lectures. I encouraged them to ask questions if they had any and additionally stayed after class to answer questions from students who may have been too shy or hesitant to ask during the lecture. I also encouraged students to come to my office to ask any further questions they may have had. I was also in charge of student affairs. Therefore, students felt an interpersonal connection with me not only as a lecturer but as a friend. They would seek advice from me, which I would provide, and they would trust my judgment enough to immediately proceed with my advice.

In teaching, it is important to have a strong conviction and to be sincere, hardworking, and strive for excellence. Treat everyone with respect. Don't take things personally, and don't take out your frustration on a student if he or she doesn't understand because it may be the teacher's fault. Teach with love and compassion and with the goal of instilling intrinsic motivation in students to allow them to appreciate the subject matter for what it is instead of getting a good grade or external rewards.

From October 1993 to October 1994, after having moved from Saudi Arabia, my life was stabilizing—my children were growing up, I had a well-paying job and loved my work, and I was surrounded by family and friends. However, during that time, Karachi was undergoing much political strife and was surrounded by daily violence. I came to the logical conclusion that this would not be the proper environment to raise my family.

As a consequence, I decided to move from Pakistan to the United States in October 1994. I would be sacrificing my established position at Baqai Hospital and leaving behind family and friends, but I believed that would the right decision. Luckily, my wife was able to provide our family with green cards because her father worked with the United States Agency of International Development. We first arrived in Los Angeles, California, where my brother-in-law lived. We stayed there for a year from October 1994 to October 1995, during which I experienced my initial struggles of moving to a new country. In order to practice medicine, I needed to take and pass the USMLE Step 1 and 2 exams to get residency. After a year of studying, I took the exam but unfortunately could not get the desired score.

On October 13, 1995, we moved to Chicago, Illinois, where my older sister lived. We lived with her for three to four weeks and then rented an apartment in November. That was a difficult time for me personally, but I needed to provide for my family. Since I could not practice medicine as a doctor, I searched for jobs to put food on the table for my family. I did not want to be stubborn or obstinate. At last, one day I was successful in obtaining a job at a grocery store for three dollars and fifty cents an hour. I did not hesitate to take up the job offer, but my family was upset because they knew I was capable of obtaining a better job. I ultimately declined the offer.

My journey continued in search of another job. In December 1995, my older sister's husband was working at O'Hare Airport as an aircraft maintenance person. He introduced me to the baggage scanner job at O'Hare Airport. Thereafter, I obtained a security job for scanning and screening luggage for five dollars an hour. This job served as the greatest source of my happiness since having become a doctor in Pakistan.

Developing Clinical Intuition as a Surgical Assistant and Leadership Intuition as Acting Supervisor of Processing and Material Management Edgewater Medical Center, Chicago, Illinois

Author's Demonstration of NBL Qualities at Edgewater Medical Center, 1996–2000

Even though I was working at O'Hare in the evenings, I would dedicate my mornings to searching for hospital jobs by visiting various hospitals in the Chicagoland area. I would visit their human resources departments to submit job applications. At last, I got an interview from the Edgewater Medical Center. I was appointed as a surgical assistant in June 17, 1996, and later was promoted to be the acting supervisor of processing and material management, where I remained until March 31, 2000.

I was appointed as surgical assistant in this medical center, where I assisted more than twenty surgeons belonging to various surgical subspecialties: vascular, cardiac, thoracic, neuro, orthopedic, podiatric, and general surgeries. Specifically, I provided the surgeons with the appropriate surgical tools to conduct their respective surgeries and even directly coordinated with the surgeon during operating procedures. As acting supervisor of processing and material management, I would also ensure that the tools were properly sterilized by staff and to ensure that the appropriate quantity and quality of materials were being used for certain surgeries.

I was also informed by the director of surgical services of different projects I could work on during my free time. I jubilantly undertook these projects as a part of my habit; I was always ready to take additional responsibility without any increase in salary. I worked closely with the director of material management to deal with various vendors to get revenue back from nearly expiring sutures used in surgery and returned less commonly used and overstocked sutures to their vendors. I took charge of the following projects and completed them in a very timely and efficient manner, saving money for the hospital:

- Had engineers replace old surgical lights, tables, and surgical instruments with new ones or had them refurbish the old ones
- Compared the cost of various surgical tools and materials across vendors to provide cheaper but effective ones to save the hospital money and to reduce the surgical operation costs for patients
- Developed a product evaluation to compare the efficacy and cost of the surgical tools and materials
- Revised and modified the types of sutures required for different surgeries and returned unused, overstocked ones
- Assessed cost-effectiveness of the use of lead aprons and thyroid shields, replacing these with more efficacious, advanced ones
- Found different qualities of materials used in implants and prosthesis to save the hospital money while maintaining effectiveness

Looking back, I definitely feel that intrinsic motivation was the primary driving force to accomplish these projects. Again, I was not being paid extra to undertake these projects, but I accepted the responsibility of these projects and did them nonetheless. They were a source of internal happiness for me. As a result of these accomplishments, the director of material management was so happy that he nominated me for Employee of the Year in 1997 for the Edgewater Medical Center, Chicago, for saving huge revenues for the hospital. To my surprise, I obtained the Employee of the Year award. This definitely served as a stepping-stone in my career after having the lows of not being able to practice medicine. It renewed my confidence and faith in my own abilities.

Research Management and Leadership Experience in the Research and Development Department (R&D) at Jesse Brown Veteran Affairs Medical Center (JBVAMC)

Author's Demonstration of NBL Qualities at Jesse Brown VAMC, 2000–Present

After my time at Edgewater, I decided to do a short stint with the Michael Reese Hospital because the material management director at Edgewater was transferred there. I worked there until I was laid off due to downsizing of employees and financial reasons. Later, I volunteered at the University of Illinois at Chicago (UIC) in a rheumatology biomedical research lab from June to December 2000. Ultimately, I accepted a part-time position at the Jesse Brown Veterans Affairs Medical Center (JBVAMC) on October 17, 2000. By December 2000, I obtained a full-time position at JBVAMC and left my volunteer position at UIC.

From October 2000 to February 2009, I was working at JBVAMC in Chicago, Illinois, as a medical administration specialist, VA Merit Review Grant administrator, human subject protocol portfolio manager, acting director of West Side Institute for Science and Education (a nonprofit organization), acting administrative officer, acting research compliance officer, research information specialist, and research coordinator for R&D committees (subcommittees: animal care and use, research safety and biosafety, and research space allocation committees).

I am currently working as a research compliance officer (RCO) since February 2009 and possess over sixteen years' hands-on experience in research management and have had to play a crucial leadership role. This role is the culmination of my various lifetime experiences. The qualities and abilities I learned during my experiences in Saudi Arabia and Pakistan have assisted me in my undertakings in the United States. They have made me who I am today—they have made me a leader.

Chapter 5

Discussion on Leadership and the Natural-Born Leader (NBL)

Personally, I think leadership entails having a certain mind-set, and this has been the case for me throughout my life. I hope to convince you that you too can achieve this mind-set because leadership boils down to being able to take actions that are in line with one's principles. I hold the belief that people are innately capable of doing anything, and it is a matter of whether they can draw out these inner qualities in light of adversity. As a leader, it is important to be able to persevere and to have confidence in your ability to tackle any challenge that comes your way.

There is no universal definition of leadership; and, indeed, it is one of the most researched areas of behavioral science that deals with organizational psychology. Since the start of civilization, people have questioned what the attributes of a successful leader are. Political scientists, philosophers, and psychologists have produced extensive literature on leadership, but despite their hard work, there is no consensus as to why and under what circumstances some people become leaders and others remain followers.

Today, leaders strive to be truly understanding of others and have a desire to build a strong culture but are often burned out due to the concomitant stresses of leading their respective organizations. I believe these leaders lack the proper mind-set to overcome these hurdles. The skills to work with our minds and our emotions and with other people are essential but rarely developed. According to Gallup 2013, leaders failed to provide genuine leadership to 70 percent of employees who were disengaged and had low productivity and innovation. Only 8 percent of people strongly agree that they experience overall well-being because of their work.

In my observation, leadership is a combination of talents and hidden skills. Research on leadership indicates that 50 to 75 percent of organizations are currently managed by people who are lacking in leadership competence. Many leadership researchers have weighed in on NBL, but, surprisingly, there is very little literature that fully explores this theory. Some research has identified some genes affecting leadership, such as the rs4950 genotype by De Neve's group.

Leadership can come in different flavors. One way to think about it is according to the differences in thinking styles, namely convergent and divergent thinking. Convergent-thinking leaders have a limited predetermined number of options and will look for data that supports one or the other. They don't consider things outside the box and, consequently, miss answers that can be equally viable or perhaps even superior. Personally, I think that this sums up the acquired-skill leaders. Acquired-skill leaders are people who just receive education and training about leadership, but they don't fully grasp the essence thereof. They are poor decision-makers because they answer problems with a narrow-minded approach and don't consider novel or unconventional options. They are focused on improving their administrative skills to run the organization, but they simultaneously lack the confidence in their own abilities to make critical decisions regarding complex situations with great success. This is because they do not have the mind-set to perform under pressure situations and hence are unable to figure out the situation, leading to a total leadership disaster.

Natural-born leaders have the ability to accomplish goals successfully, and they have hidden skills to achieve any target easily. In my experience, they have a unique ability to deal with stressful situations honestly, confidently, and intuitively and are creative, knowledgeable, charismatic, and sociable. The NBL has the following general abilities and qualities: verbal fluency, proper judgment, responsibility, active participation, achievement, versatility, vigor, and the ability to influence others. One person can play this role and make a difference. The NBL has certain traits that contribute to efficient and effective leadership in all situations. I firmly believe that personal characteristics, behaviors, and hidden skills play a crucial role in bringing out this form of leadership.

There is a popular saying that "leaders are not born; they are made." But in many ways, leadership can also manifest itself naturally. We've all heard the term "natural-born leader," and we might have used it to describe our boss, our colleagues, and even some of our peers. But what makes a leader "natural"? What makes a natural-born leader different from the other types of leader? What specific characteristics do these natural-born leaders possess?

I have a strong belief that we all have some hidden qualities that need to be discovered in order to find our natural leadership qualities. The natural-born leader possesses a set of instincts. And so what I mean is that leadership is not just a behavior—it is a mind-set. And until it is natural, one's success as a leader will be limited.

Why Do I Think That I Am a Natural-Born leader?

I believe that I have become a natural-born leader, which I will illustrate through my personal experiences from August 1967 through February 2017. During these last fifty years of my life, I have come across several challenges and hardships that I was able to control and mange confidently with great degrees of success due to my natural-born leadership qualities. I noticed that I would never be under any stress or pressure during these situations. I would always stay calm and confident. Under those situations, people around me would ask how I managed to combat the adversities so successfully. I always tell them that it is only due to optimism and confidence in my own abilities.

No one is born perfect in this world, but in due time, we overcome our mistakes, increasing perfection in our careers as we are cornered to make difficult decisions to progress and succeed in life. In my estimation, human beings were created with many hidden qualities and characteristics, which they start using in their lifetime even without any education. I grew up in a developing country where the majority of people are illiterate. Nonetheless, I still knew many high-functioning individuals with no formal training who were running great businesses. This came to show me that there was something natural about leadership that could be taught in a classroom but was rather cultivated from within. When one thinks of a leader, the first thing that comes to mind is a political leader or any successful CEO or entrepreneur; but my focus is on the natural-born leader. The majority of people think that a third of all leaders have intrinsic leadership qualities, and the remaining two-thirds obtain these qualities extrinsically through training.

However, despite this statistic, I believe that the number of natural-born leaders is much higher than those that attain leadership skills through training. People born with leadership qualities are most successful in their life because of their strong decision-making capabilities in time-sensitive, pressured situations and their strong vision and forethought. They have no fear in making decisions because they are not afraid of failure. Upon experiencing failure, they self-analyze the errors in their decision-making process and come back with innovative ideas and a stronger determination to resolve the situation. They have tasted the bitterness of failure and have a desire to taste the sweetness of success. After experiencing success, an indescribable pleasure overcomes them, giving them strength to move further in that direction. I have a strong belief that the progress in this world is made because of the uncanny abilities of these natural-born leaders. Natural-born leaders are always firm in their decision-making due to the confidence in their own abilities and their vision of the future in successfully accomplishing short-term and long-term goals.

Since my childhood, whenever I was assigned a task to perform at home or at work, I would never say no. From a young age, I had realized that I was always ready to accept any type of challenge. I would have the goal of accomplishing challenges with a high degree of efficiency and in a timely manner, regardless of their difficulty. This mind-set is the bread and butter of the natural-born leader.

When not assigned to perform a task and noticing that a particular task needed to be performed, I did not wait for someone to tell me to take charge. Instead, I myself would go and provide any extra help. I personally derive great pleasure and happiness when helping others. It truly invigorates me, motivating me to tackle other tasks and projects. I would describe this feeling as similar to that which one feels after exercising, in which endorphins, serotonin, and norepinephrine increase one's feeling of pleasure.

I further attribute my success to the level of confidence I have when confronted with daily tasks. I have a daily work agenda involving a series of targets, or aims, that I hope to accomplish that day. After successfully accomplishing a target in a timely manner, I brim with confidence due to the self-assurance I receive that I can indeed execute tasks efficiently. This results in a domino effect; I am immediately ready for the next target because of this self-assurance that I have built after accomplishing my previous target.

I also try to spend more time listening to others' opinions when appropriate and to assess their opinion in the context of the issue or task on hand to make well-informed decisions moving forward.

I am always open to new ways of doing things. I have a strong ability to learn from my past mistakes and the courage to make better decisions. I always consider and try multiple options before finding the most optimal one. I am not afraid to be original and always ask questions for more clarity. I never stop learning. Every day, I am learning from my surroundings and even from my children. I always try to remain focused on my daily agenda of tasks.

A sign of a truly great leader is the success of the team underneath them. This is my strength, and I want to accomplish work by any means on time and with great success—nothing less than 100 percent, which is my goal all the time.

Furthermore, I have possessed clinical intuition through my work as a physician and a nonclinical intuition through my experience as a research compliance officer and administrator. This pair of intuitions has allowed me to make decisions in novel circumstances—those in which I have no prior experience. As I have noticed in my career on so many occasions, I am very good in finding immediate solutions for complex issues, yielding strong, positive outcomes. My experiences have built my intuition, allowing me to have epiphanies when searching for solutions. To me, it feels as natural as breathing.

Aristotle once said that "quality is not an act, it is a habit." These habits are learned through interactions with our environment on a daily basis. The various attributes I have described above can be encapsulated by the following qualities: insightfulness and self-confidence, intrinsic motivation, integrity and unlocking trust, communication, sacrifice, patience and composure, open-mindedness, courage, compassion, and optimism. These qualities are imperative to becoming an NBL and thus vital for success. I will articulate how I uncovered these qualities within me through my various life experiences and hope you introspect and recall your life experiences to uncover and draw these qualities within yourself.

Chapter 6

Cultivation of My Natural-Born Leader Qualities

What Is Intuition?

Intuition is a very abstract concept and is difficult to describe. I think I would do it injustice by providing a one-line definition from the dictionary. In my observation, intuition entails having an instinct that is subconsciously developed through the various experiences one undergoes in life. I feel that if I have seen a particular situation once, then that experience will allow me to better manage and handle different, unrelated situations down the line without ever having seen that situation.

What Is Clinical Intuition?

There are various kinds of intuition. One kind of intuition I developed through my experience as a physician was, of course, clinical intuition. Clinical intuition is also difficult to describe. Personally, it is the art of integrating nonverbal information that a patient presents with in order to reach a diagnosis, reducing the need for diagnostic testing. This is especially important in children, who often react differently to procedures, tests, and other treatment modalities. Medicine is as much an art as it is a science, and this skill is definitely the former.

When I started implementing my clinical intuition, I really began to enjoy treating patients. On several occasions, I even avoided invasive, costly procedures by making accurate on-the-spot diagnoses and treating the patient conservatively with pharmacotherapy and lifestyle changes before considering a more aggressive treatment.

In the practice of medicine, a holistic approach to patient care is often touted—one that not only focuses on the disease but the whole individual. How can such a lofty goal be accomplished? The most skilled physician is the one who has the strongest observational skills in detecting clinical signs. These signs include behavior, appearance, and other observable signs. The clinical assessment begins as soon as an individual walks into the office. His or her gait, appearance, and mood—all these tiny things provide a wealth of information to the physician in the treatment of the patient, especially a child, who is more vulnerable to emotional stress. These skills together comprise, in part, clinical intuition, which can help us realize the ideal of holistic patient care.

According to Albert Einstein, "The intuitive mind is a sacred gift and the rational mind is a faithful servant. We have created a society that honors the servant and has forgotten the gift."

Can Intuition Be Learned?
Insightfulness and Self-Confidence

No. Just kidding. You too can learn intuition! It is all about making the most of your experiences in life. The prerequisite of intuition is having a base knowledge of that subject. If you have a solid background of the issue on hand, your mind will start processing various unique solutions for these issues. Informed intuition will develop if you think of yourself as a leader. This will build a level of insightfulness, entailing a deep understanding of the task being accomplished, which will only reinforce this intuition in a continuous cycle. This cycle will ultimately result in well-informed decision-making and positive outcomes. When observing the fruits of your decision-making, it will only serve to build self-confidence—a quality essential to leadership. The following flow chart illustrates this dynamic.

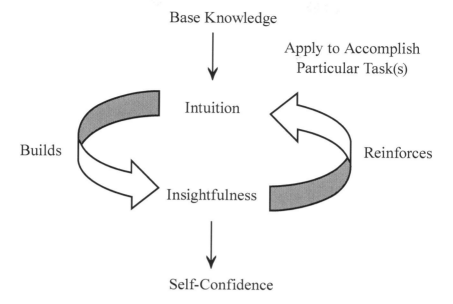

Base Knowledge

Apply to Accomplish
Particular Task(s)

Intuition

Builds

Reinforces

Insightfulness

Self-Confidence

"Self-confidence" is a term that is used to define how we feel about our ability to perform challenging tasks whether they have value or not, but in my case, I always take tasks seriously, regardless of their value. This, I believe, is pivotal to fostering my self-confidence. There is always a possibility of making mistakes, which is inevitable especially when doing something new.

Self-confidence includes knowing what to do when mistakes come and how to make corrections. Therefore, it narrows down to problem-solving and decision-making. The real test of self-confidence rises when confronted with making high-risk decisions. You can handle this situation by better planning and by thinking about various options (productive and nonproductive) to resolve this situation, and be prepared for the unknown situation. Self-confidence is a function of successful risk-taking. In this way, everyone will achieve something.

In leaders, self-confidence is more important than skill, knowledge, or even experience. Lead meetings with authority, get people to communicate with you candidly, and be open to feedback, particularly when it is of the constructive type. Without self-confidence, you will second-guess your decisions, find yourself becoming defensive when challenged, and become a follower.

I used my insightfulness and self-confidence in Saudi Arabia during hospital meetings by making crucial, hospital-wide decisions and took that hospital to the next level, essentially making it a model hospital in the region. I felt happy to see the fruition of my vision and received positive feedback and encouragement. I had an internal desire to do more for the hospital staff, patients, and the MOH. I felt relaxed and happy even during challenging situations. I was taking calculated risks and learning from my mistakes. I think self-confidence is one of the main characteristics of charisma. I was more assertive and effective in my administrative leadership role. But at the same time, I recognized my weaknesses and never thought of myself as superior to others. Remember, nobody is perfect. There I was, always ready to learn from others. I was always appreciating hospital staff for doing a good job.

In my case, I noticed that insightfulness and self-confidence enhanced my decision-making ability and contributed to my internal happiness, which has allowed me to become an NBL. I will provide various examples of how I built insightfulness and self-confidence.

One of the first instances when I felt that I developed and demonstrated these two qualities was in Karachi, Pakistan. I remember that I was roughly four to five months into my residency at the time, working the night shift in Dr. Rizvi's urology ward at the civil hospital. I was in charge of covering all inpatients in the urology ward and the ER in addition to being the emergency, on-call resident that night, covering other departments of the hospital. It was Dr. Rizvi's policy that only one resident would cover the entire department from 7:00 p.m. to 7:00 a.m. and had permission to call the following individuals depending on the severity of the patient case, in this order: the registrar, assistant professor, associate professor, and Dr. Rizvi.

One summer night around one o'clock, I received a call from the ER to assess a middle-aged male patient who was admitted to the ER after having his abdominal area crushed by being run over by a truck. The patient was in critical condition, having lost excessive blood. As a urology resident, my job was to exclude any collateral damage to the kidneys, ureter, or bladder and hence rule out the need of surgery. Through my assessment, I determined that the kidneys, ureter, and bladder were indeed intact by passing Foley's catheter to check blood in the urine, so I gave clearance to general surgery to do a laparotomy to treat his abdominal injuries. The surgeon took this critical patient into the operating room for surgery, and I returned to the urology ward to tend the more critical renal failure patients and ensured that the nurse carried out orders for surgical procedures the following morning.

The next morning around seven o'clock, Dr. Rizvi arrived at the urology ward and was sitting with all the other departmental staff members in the conference room. As I entered the room, he asked me, "Did you see the patient with the crushed abdomen last night in ER?"

I was ambivalent as to why he asked, so I responded, "Did I do something wrong?"

Dr. Rizvi chuckled and told me that the surgeon met him in the elevator and inquired if there was a Dr. Salar. Dr. Rizvi told him that "Dr. Salar is our new resident."

The surgeon, surprised, remarked, "I have never seen a doctor with such strong confidence in such a critical situation to ascertain that there were no injuries to the patient's urological areas." Then the surgeon asked Dr. Rizvi, "Did he call you at night or any other senior staff?"

Dr. Rizvi said, "He did not call anyone because I gave him the opportunity to work independently and make his own decisions." Dr. Rizvi was very happy with my performance. Looking back, I never called any senior doctor at night when I was working alone with complicated renal failure patients, conducting peritoneal dialysis and hemodialysis, and cases of septic shock, metabolic acidosis/alkalosis, respiratory failure, cardiac arrest, and uremic coma, to list a few.

That one year, urology residency was a career game changer for me. By giving me the freedom to independently treat and manage urology patients during the night shift, I developed my clinical intuition. By handling a broad array of urology cases, I developed my insightfulness and built the confidence to handle more severe and critical cases. All of this was reinforced by making cognizant decisions and receiving words of encouragement from my preceptor. It felt natural to me, and this essence trickled into my personality. I would never panic at the time of managing a dying patient with paramedical staff. I knew what my role was and what was needed from the nurses. I would take responsibility, rely on my intuition and insight, and command the situation with confidence. The paramedical staff was very content with my work and enjoyed working with me due to my calm disposition during these high-pressure situations. That is what I had seen Dr. Rizvi do when dealing with his patients, always treating them with love and care as well as doing his best to save his patients' lives.

After one year of urology residency, I started my next residency in the Internal Medicine Unit II at the Civil Hospital. In 1982, I memorably recall one night when I noticed a middle-aged male patient who was suffering from hypochondriasis, in which patients get health anxiety. The patient believed he had some form of organ failure despite normal vitals, physical examination, and blood work. The nurse was instructed by the attending to inject valium intravenously to relax the patient. He was not one of the patients on my panel, but I watched from afar due to my curiosity in the case. While the nurse was injecting the valium, the patient suddenly went into cardiac arrest. The nurse panicked and immediately yelled, "The patient is dead!" I was in the vicinity, so I responded to her call and promptly started cardiopulmonary resuscitation. The nurse acknowledged that she injected the valium too quickly, which we concluded to be the cause of the cardiac arrest. Fortunately, the patient's vitals returned to baseline, and the EKG showed normal sinuses and rhythm within five to ten minutes without any residual complication of the cardiac arrest.

I managed that patient alone with two nurses because my confidence had prevailed. I could have very easily called the registrar, attending physician, or other physicians who were on-call, but I understood the severity of the situation and needed to take immediate action. I used the insight I acquired from my previous cardiac arrest cases as a urology resident and held my composure to appropriately and successfully treat the patient.

In 1991, I was working as the attending internist and pulmonologist at the Al-Jihad Hospital in Mecca. Every year in Saudi Arabia, physicians across the country were sent to Mecca on hajj duty for a six-week period to work at the Al-Jihad Hospital because millions of pilgrims across the world congregate to Mecca during this period for a religious pilgrimage. As one can imagine, it concomitantly led to an increase in demand of patient care during this span.

In the beginning, I was working in the heat stroke unit before being transferred to the medical ward. I vividly remember my first day in that ward. I saw twenty patients in that room. Scanning the other corner of the room, my eyes immediately focused on one young male patient, about twenty years old, who was laid on a bed in an opisthotonus position. I made a swift on-the-spot diagnosis of a tetanus infection from afar and approached him, taking his past medical history and examining him. The patient appeared alert and oriented. There were no signs of any strychnine poisoning, trauma, or open sores, which could serve as entry points for an infection.

I do not know what happened to me next, but I had an epiphany that he may have third-degree hemorrhoids because many of these pilgrims during hajj lived in tents in Minna, a city near Mecca, and these tents were not the most sanitary of places. In addition, it was the norm to use water to clean genital areas after urination and defecation, which may have served as a source of infection. So I asked him if he had any hemorrhoids, and he was astonished and responded, "Yes!" He reported that he had bleeding and painful hemorrhoids onset the last several days, and he even had to use his finger to push these protruding hemorrhoids back. Now I felt confident in my diagnosis of tetanus infection. The bacteria had entered the body through his infected bleeding hemorrhoids. His opisthotonus posture was due to the tetanus bacteria attacking his nervous system, resulting in severe hyperextension and spasticity of head, neck, and spinal column muscles.

By excluding any other differential diagnosis, I began treatment of his tetanus immediately with antibiotics and antitetanus serum. The patient was then referred to a nearby infectious disease hospital for management under isolation. His diagnosis of tetanus infection was ascertained the following day in the hospital.

In the example above, I used my clinical intuition to make an on-the-spot diagnosis and start treatment immediately. For all intents and purposes, the patient may have had some other infection, in which I would have been liable for starting him on the wrong therapy. However, I had the utmost faith in my intuition and decision-making to quickly and effectively treat the patient. This quality, I feel, is imperative for leaders to instill and encapsulate because as a leader one must make prompt decisions, and any hesitancy will show lack of confidence from taking appropriate action. It is my firm belief that if one's intention is good, the cure will come from another source. While there is a possibility it may be a wrong decision, a decision is better than no decision at all. Making wrong decisions will also reinforce your intuition and prevent you from making similar mistakes in like scenarios down the line.

Intrinsic Motivation: Path to Pleasure and Happiness

Intrinsic motivation is the desire to accomplish tasks or do activities based on internal rewards as opposed to accomplishing them on a reward-punishment basis. It is a difficult concept to describe because this motivation does not manifest itself physically, but it is something that comes from within and varies from person to person. It rudimentarily entails doing something for the sake of it and deriving some form of pleasure or happiness from it.

In my case, I was always willing to tackle additional projects and take responsibility for matters that were not directly under my belt because I gained internal pleasure and happiness from doing these activities. Successfully carrying out these additional tasks supplemented my desire to do something more and to do something extraordinary, making the impossible possible. As a natural-born leader, it is necessary to have this element of intrinsic motivation.

When I was teaching at Baqai Medical College, I recall one of my students—whom I will refer to with the alias Shahid—who came to my office hours in March 1994 because he was immensely struggling in my class. As an instructor, my primary responsibility was, of course, to educate my students and assist them in whatever way possible in their medical studies. I was open to having students ask me questions during and after class and in office hours. However, Shahid seemed like a special case because it was not a medical question, like, "What signs and symptoms does a patient with asthma present with versus a patient with COPD?" He came to me with conflicting desires on why he was pursuing the field to begin with rather than asking me a clinically related question. I needed to understand his desire and motive to study medicine. As a physician, teacher, and leader, I felt obliged to put him on the right track moving forward.

Instead of educating him on studying more, changing his study habits, or paying more attention in class, I asked him, "Why do you want to pursue medicine?" He responded with the fact that he came from an affluent family and belonged to what is considered a high social class in Pakistan. He also told me that he wanted to pursue further medical education and practice in Britain or the United States. When I asked him what his medical interests were, he beat around the bush, stating that he wanted to do internal medicine or family medicine. I figured he lacked sincerity in his pursuit of medicine because it seemed from our conversation that he was in it for the money instead of understanding medical conditions and treating patients with the breadth of medical and clinical skills he would acquire in the medical training process.

I spent the next thirty to forty minutes discussing the field of medicine with him. I informed him that he could go to a different profession if his target was to earn money. After becoming a doctor in a country such as Pakistan, we have a responsibility to take care of poor people coming from agricultural areas and poverty-stricken villages—people who cannot always afford treatment costs. As a doctor, we should always be ready to sacrifice our time, money, and sleep. It is a noble profession, not a business. Especially in Pakistan, we were fortunate enough to have the base amount of food, shelter, and the basic necessities of life to get by.

I asked, "Do you think, after getting a lot of money, your life will be filled with all kinds of luxury? What if after obtaining all these luxuries, your desire to obtain more is insatiable, and you want more? Will you be happy then? It will get to the point that having this extra money will cause you more stress, anxiety, and sleep loss. You will have the desire to compete with your colleagues to determine who can earn more money in the medical profession."

At this point, he opened up to me, informing me that his parents suffered from anxiety and depression in spite of all the luxury they have and that they take antidepressants to treat their symptoms. I saw the guilt in his eyes, and it appeared that he wanted to amend his ways. "Now tell me, do you want to undergo the same suffering as your parents?"

I recounted to him my example back in Saudi Arabia, when I left my status as hospital director and chief of medicine at the Al-Midhnab Hospital to do what I thought was best for my family and to take care of our nation's people. If I wanted money, I could have stayed indefinitely in Saudi Arabia, but my top priority was not money. It was instead to obtain a state of internal happiness. I further advised him to not focus on his grade, indicative of his performance in the class, but to instead focus on obtaining a mastery of the material on hand. "Grades and other external rewards will come, but what is most important is the end goal: knowing how to treat and care for a patient whether they are complaining of cough or having the fortitude, resolve, and confidence to manage more critical patients."

My words resonated with him, and he promised me that he would get his priorities straight and that he was determined to focus more on getting an understanding and appreciation of medicine.

I gently advised Shahid to come meet with me from time to time to transform his negative thinking and steer it toward optimism and toward the beauty of the field of medicine. He promised me that he would follow my advice. At a follow-up meeting, I noticed his eyes were beaming, and his demeanor showed positivity and a genuine desire to serve others.

That encounter was fueled by my intrinsic motivation to help that student. I did not physically gain a reward from our meeting, nor was it really within my bounds to give him a motivational speech.

There were about a hundred other medical students in the class, and to some, my time could have been better spent going over lecture material. Instead, I chose to discuss this matter with him, hoping to observe a change in his demeanor toward medicine.

Integrity: Unlocking Trust

Integrity is one of the most difficult leadership characteristics to teach because it necessarily entails having honesty, while upholding moral and ethical values. As leaders, the ability to demonstrate this quality is imperative to unlocking trust among your followers and those you lead. While being honest simply entails telling the truth, integrity goes one step beyond that and considers the various underpinnings and factors that affect this truth and its impetus upon the person to whom this truth is told. It shows that you have genuine concern for the other person and strong moral righteousness.

During my clinical experiences, integrity was essential to building trust among patients. Having seen many patient cases, it was easy to succumb to the likely reality that many of my critical patients would either not survive or would need highly invasive procedures to return their health to baseline. However, I felt determined to never cover up bad news and to contemplate all possible solutions to their problems, taking into strong consideration their personal and socioeconomic background. In this same vein, it is also important to maintain a level of transparency with patients, which necessitates honesty with good moral character. This, I believe, is the formula to developing lasting relationships with not only those whom you lead but also by extension the people you meet in life.

In April 1990, I was working as an internist and pulmonologist at the Al-Midhnab Hospital and vividly recall a surgery case. The patient was a thirty-five-year-old male Egyptian farmer who presented with gangrene due to a poisonous snake bite he received on his left lower leg two weeks prior to hospitalization. The surgeon had called me for consultation to give him preoperational clearance to do a below-the-knee amputation of the patient's left leg. The patient recounted his snake bite, which he reported that he received while working on the farm and recalled a "burning sensation" with the bite mark and bleeding and saw a snake slither away. He told me that he went to his primary doctor initially for treatment and was later told to come to the hospital for further evaluation and treatment. He had a destitute upbringing, and I recognized that he had come far from his hometown to get this treatment.

Upon physical examination, on the medial side of his left lower leg, roughly six to eight inches above the ankle joint, it appeared dark, discolored with gangrene, had 2+ edema, and surrounding redness, indicative of an infection. This examination gave me an idea of what the most suitable treatment therapy would be for his leg, and I was confident that he would make full recovery in the next forty-eight to seventy-two hours without needing an amputation. In light of this, I explained to the patient that he would not need surgery—at least for the time being. I informed him that I would treat his wound by debriding it and injecting a poly snake antivenom and antibiotic. After explaining this to the patient, he looked into my eyes and gave me consent.

I immediately started treatment. I asked the nurse to bring a sterile surgical kit for minor debridement and used it to make an incision in the surrounding area and to drain any potential infectious materials. I then cleaned the wound with an aseptic solution, leaving it open to the aerobic environment. I proceeded to inject antitetanus serum, snake poly-venom vaccine and an antibiotic to control the infection.

The surgeon was not too keen on the idea. "The poison will cover fast. He won't live." These were the things he kept telling me. But I had a different plan. I wanted to give my plan a chance. He was furious. But my heart wouldn't waver. "How can you be so insane?"

I remember him saying. "Do you not care about the patient's life?" Of course I did. Of course I did. That's why I couldn't just send my patient to surgery. He was an Egyptian who worked in the fields as a laborer. He wasn't rich. He had a family and kids. What would become of him if his leg was amputated? How could he work? How could his family survive? This world can be cruel and uncaring.

I remember feeling a sense of hopelessness at the situation, but at the same time a sense of responsibility. "Please," I prayed, "if there is a way to save this man, grant him a cure, God." I explained the situation to the man. The honest answer would have been to abide by the surgeon's orders and inform him that he would need amputation, but I persevered. He put his life in my hands, saying he trusted me. I compromised with the surgeon, saying that I was taking responsibility for the patient, and if there was any worsening of his condition, I would send for immediate surgical amputation.

Thereafter, I carefully monitored this patient three to four times a day for the next couple of days. Almost miraculously, after forty-eight hours, his gangrenous leg started healing. I continued treatment for ten days until complete recovery. With tears in his eyes, the patient thanked me for saving him from amputation and lifelong disability.

I took a risk when it came to treat his gangrenous leg, but it was a risk worth taking because I held true to my principles and saved that man's leg from amputation. I tenaciously held on to my integrity in that critical, time-sensitive situation and came out of it successful, having developed a bond with this patient. I took a chance, came out ahead, and did not have to compromise my moral principles.

Communication: Importance of Listening and Observation

Communication is the art of conveying information between two or more parties. It necessitates listening to what others have to say and relying on keen observational skills to recognize nonverbal cues to come up with appropriate responses. This is particularly important in the medical field and epitomizes the doctor-patient relationship. In my experience as a physician, this relationship is fortified via communication. By communicating successfully with patients, they will develop trust and be open up to you. They may bring up seemingly disparate or irrelevant pieces of information about their life, but this information may actually be pivotal to finding the right diagnosis and best treatment option under the umbrella of that patient's unique circumstances. Communication is also important between employees at any given workplace to ensure that their work operates with flow.

One day in 1992 at the Al-Midhnab Hospital, I was passing by the operating room and saw that nurses were taking a twenty-nine-year-old male patient to the operating room in a hurry. I asked the nurses about the case. They told me that it was a case of acute appendicitis that was nearing rupture, and the surgeon wanted immediate surgery to remove his appendix. However, upon observing the patient's facial expression, it did not seem like he was suffering from acute appendicitis. To me, it seemed as if the patient was exaggerating the amount of pain he was in. I interjected with the nurses and asked if I could examine the patient outside the operating room. I distracted the patient by conversing with him as I palpated his lower abdomen. I did not note any swelling or tenderness indicative of appendicitis. If it was appendicitis, the patient would have shrieked in pain. I informed him that he did not have appendicitis and told him that having an appendectomy may cause further, unnecessary complications. He opened up to me and informed me that he had an argument with his girlfriend on telephone and developed the abdominal pain soon after that.

My diagnosis was a hysterical conversion reaction that manifested itself as abdominal pain. I informed the surgeon, writing very clearly on the patient's chart that no surgical intervention was required. I admitted the patient under internal medicine and my supervision. I treated him with valium through slow IV fluid injection and advised routine lab tests to exclude any other illness. The next day, I provided relaxation and behavioral therapy and discharged the patient in good health.

I used my strong observational skills in a matter of a few seconds to rule out acute appendicitis and prevent unnecessary surgery. By using communication as a distraction, I observed his response to the palpation of his lower abdomen and noted no tenderness. As a leader, it is important not only to listen to what others have to say, but to recognize their nonverbal cues, the expression on their faces, and tone of their voices to make well-informed decisions moving forward. The surgeon was not happy, but I took responsibility and did what was best for the patient. It was also tough decision, but my intuition and observational skills led me to take appropriate action.

Sacrifice

The biggest part of my success is accepting challenges and doing additional projects without expecting any reward (i.e., sacrifice). Wherever I have worked during my career, I have always performed duties beyond my job description, taking on additional responsibilities at work for the betterment of the organization.

I went through the process of becoming a doctor, which required special training and the same with certain expectations as it pertained to my job. A *job* is an activity that an individual performs in exchange for payment while *work* is an activity that an individual performs in order to produce or accomplish something. "Work" is a general term that refers to all activities that one does, while "job" is more specific. When one is hired for a job, he has to get into a contract with his employer, and he has to abide by the regulations of the company. In a job, the goals and targets are more specific and well laid out for the employees to follow and achieve. The term "work" is the most commonly used word in our day-to-day life; it refers to the activities performed by us so as to achieve the desired outcome. The majority of people understand that the meaning of "job" is to do a required list of activities for a certain period of time and as ordained in their job description. This is done to protect them from being fired and get a regularly paid salary. These groups of people are not flexible, never volunteer for additional work at their jobs, and hesitate to participate in new changes unless additional compensation will be offered.

In June 1992, a fifty-year-old male patient came to my clinic with a recent history of fevers, fatigue, and weight loss onset three to four months prior. Upon examination and doing lab work, his hemoglobin was low, indicating that he was anemic; and I noticed an enlarged liver and spleen upon palpation. He informed me that he was staying in the desert during vacation, which was a norm in Saudi Arabia as desert nights in the summer would be cool, providing comfort from the hot weather during the day. My first suspicion was visceral leishmaniasis because his symptoms and enlargement of liver and spleen indicated that he may have this infection. In addition, leishmaniasis is transmitted through the bite of infected female sand flies, which are found in deserts. These sand flies inject infective agents into their host's blood upon biting. This further supported my diagnosis.

In light of this information, I called the orthopedic surgeon to perform a bone marrow aspiration biopsy, which allowed us to visualize these potential infectious agents, called amastigotes, indicative of leishmaniasis. We asked the pathologist to examine the bone marrow biopsy under a microscope, and he confirmed my diagnosis by identifying these amastigotes. If the disease was not treated immediately, it could have been fatal for the patient. I decided to treat this patient with pentavalent antimonial, such as sodium stibogluconate. I called the pharmacy about this drug, but it was not in the Ministry of Health's formulary and thus not available.

I refused to let the patient go untreated. I decided to go to a private pharmacy about two kilometers from the hospital later that night and spent 117 Saudi riyal, the official Saudi currency, to purchase the pentavalent antimonial drug. I had the patient come the following day, and I administered the treatment. I had this patient follow up with me after a few weeks. The patient's condition returned to baseline as his symptoms improved and his affected organs returned to normal size.

Looking back, I did not care that I was sacrificing my own money to treat my patient. I knew it was the morally right thing to do and that I would ultimately be holding true to my personal principles. The patient fully recovered from the disease and was able to return to doing his daily activities. This gave me internal pleasure and happiness because I was able to make such a significant impact for the patient through my sacrifice.

In September 1992, I remember a seventeen-year-old male patient who presented with a scorpion sting. He informed me that a big black scorpion had stung him. I admitted him to the ICU from the ER at around 11:30 p.m., anticipating serious complications. I immediately started antiscorpion sting treatment, including vaccines, with other supportive management. The ER was very busy that night, and I was the on-call doctor, so I went to go check up on some of my other patients in the meanwhile. With the possibility of his condition deteriorating, I promised to return in one hour and told the nurse to contact me as soon as his symptoms worsened or new symptoms manifested. After an hour, as soon as I went back to the ICU, the nurse told me that she was about to page me because the patient was vomiting and started bleeding from all his orifices, including through vomiting, coughing, and through his nose and rectum. Upon arriving in his room, he was in critical condition and gasping. I called the anesthetic to insert an endotracheal tube and told the nurse to arrange blood for potential transfusion. I began emergency treatment and needed at least five to six hours so that the antiscorpion treatment would work and thus needed to keep his vital signs stable. I knew the patient could die soon with the way he presented, but I persevered, only focusing on the task in front of me. I really had to use the knowledge from all my previous experiences to treat him. I spent the whole night with this patient, and finally after seven in the morning, the patient opened his eyes and became stable, and his bleeding stopped.

While I sacrificed my money in the previous example, I sacrificed my time in this one because I, of course, had other critical patients to monitor, but knew I had to do something urgently to save that boy's life. I spent my time all night to tend to that patient even though I only served as a consult. That experience also gave me the confidence to deal with critical, life-and-death patient cases in the future. Sacrifice on my end produced life-saving outcomes for my patients. I chose to do additional work because it was the right thing to do, instead of choosing to only abide by my job description.

Patience and Composure

Patience entails having the ability to tolerate, withstand, or refrain from doing a certain action or behavior without getting frustrated, anxious, or worried. As human beings, our patience is tested on a daily basis. Whether it is waiting for any given red light to turn green when driving, waiting for hot or cold water to come out of a faucet, or anxiously waiting to meet a famous celebrity, patience plays a pivotal role. In our fast-paced lives, we have to process so much old and new information daily that sometimes it is very difficult to maintain our patience. The ultimate consequence of losing our patience is that we start to become very anxious about any particular situation we are confronted with and come up with hasty, ill-informed solutions to circumvent waiting for it.

As a leader, patience is the key to making well-informed decisions because you have the power; you hold the switch to making decisions and delivering commands on demand. If leaders do not consider the cost-benefit analysis of a certain decision, then they are blindly making decisions that could have severe repercussions for those that these decisions affect.

As a physician, patience is, of course, very important, as we must step back from patient cases, carefully culminating and analyzing the information we have on them to find the proper diagnosis. We have to wait for reports from the hospitals they were hospitalized at and from labs, imaging centers, and other providers. All this information plays a pertinent role in deciding what the assessment, plan, and treatment of that particular patient is moving forward. However, there are times where it is simply difficult to be patient. For instance, if a patient is having a cardiac arrest, he or she only has two to three minutes for resuscitation lest they get permanent brain damage, kidney damage, or even death.

In May 1989, I was seeing a sixty-year-old female patient who was referred to me from a surgical clinic for medical clearance to do a cholecystectomy. She weighed over three hundred pounds and had type 2 diabetes mellitus, asthma, essential hypertension, and congestive heart failure. She complained of nausea, vomiting, and right upper abdominal pain, onset on and off for years and upon eating any food high in fats. Her previous providers refused to assess that patient for medical clearance to do a cholecystectomy because they were afraid to take responsibility, knowing she was a high-risk patient for the procedure due to her comorbidities and morbid obesity.

I decided to take charge and was determined to clear her for surgery. I evaluated her and ordered lab tests, an EKG, and nebulizer treatment in addition to an oral bronchodilator to control asthma. I also changed the dosage of her antihypertensive medication. I followed up with her one week later to reevaluate her status. One week after reviewing all her lab and diagnostic test results and noting that her lungs were clear to auscultation bilaterally, I provided the patient with preoperational medical clearance for elective surgery with a special note of giving her anesthesia to manage her asthma during the surgery to prevent any pulmonary complications. I also informed the anesthesiologist to contact me from the operating room for further management if any respiratory complications arose. The surgeon approved my clearance and scheduled her for surgery.

I remember that the day of her surgery I was on standby, and immediately, the surgeon who performed the cholecystectomy approached me, brought his arms out wide, and gave me a hug. I was startled. "I never saw such a brave physician like you in my life. In this hospital, she was coming for the last two years, and no attending physician was ready to give her clearance for surgery. Due to her comorbidities, many were afraid to give clearance." He asked, "How did you clear her for surgery?"

I said, "When I examined this patient for medical clearance, I noticed she was experiencing nausea, vomiting, and abdominal pain due to her multiple gallstones. As long as I managed her complications, surgery would be fine."

He once again commended my patience and risk in clearing the patient for surgery. I continued her postoperative medical treatment in the surgical ward. During that span, she held out her hands and thanked me immensely for ameliorating her quality of life. The surgeon discharged her ten days later in stable condition and had her follow up with me on a monthly cadence to follow up on her comorbidities. I was able to move forward from this case with my head held high, knowing that I had made the right decision.

I approached the case very patiently and in a stepwise fashion. The patient's quality of life was poor, and that's why I felt the need to do something. I didn't simply rule the patient as unfit for the cholecystectomy. I had genuine concern for her and wanted to give her immediate relief, noticing her gastrointestinal symptoms and concomitant suffering, but I also knew that this was not a case that I could solve after a quick twenty-minute visit or even in a few days. It would take some time. By using a methodic approach, I was able to come up with a well-informed assessment plan to get her ready for preoperational clearance and alleviated her chronic suffering by finally clearing her for surgery.

That optimism encapsulated the way I approached patients for years to come. In February 1993, a fifty-eight-year-old female patient was brought to the ER at around 6:00 a.m., presenting with two fox bites and multiple scratches all over her face and hands. She explained that it happened about an hour ago when she was sleeping in a tent with her family. It was Saudi custom to sleep in the desert in tents during long weekends. Unfortunately, on this one particular weekend, a fox suddenly entered the tent and attacked this woman. Luckily, her son was also nearby; he hit the fox on the head with a strong wooden rod, killing it.

I had never until this point seen a patient presenting to the hospital after having been attacked by a fox, so this was an unusual case for me. Nonetheless, I first obtained the patient's medical history and simultaneously did a physical examination. The first plan of action was to clean the two bite marks and scratches using soap and water— to avoid any infection, like rabies. I dressed the wound with fresh bandages and instructed the patient to change the wound dressings every couple of days to prevent infection. The wound was dressed in fresh bandaging every couple of days to prevent infection. Fox bites are very painful. Therefore, I gave her analgesics for pain relief and administered five injections of prophylaxes (i.e., antirabies serum) to her abdomen.

Since she was at a high risk of developing rabies infection, we had to wait at least ten days to get the fox's postmortem brain report and its saliva to ascertain or rule out any active rabies in the fox. The son was intelligent enough to bring the dead fox to the hospital. I prepared a report of this incident and handed it, along with the dead fox, to the police, who would send it to the Al-Midhnab Health Department for postmortem analysis. To diagnose rabies, the fox's brain would show Negri bodies, indicative of rabies. The report came in after ten days, showing no trace of rabies, and the patient was cleared to go. I knew I had to wait, but as a physician, I was concerned that she might actually have rabies or some other infection requiring prompt treatment. I wanted to make sure we did whatever was necessary and as soon as possible to treat her, as she could be suffering from rabies. This case truly taught me the value of patience and that we cannot expect immediate solutions to the problems we face in life.

In the same vein as patience, composure plays a complementary role as a leader. Composure is the quality of being calm under stressful situations and having control over one's emotions during these situations. These situations are usually uncommon, but when they do occur, they can induce a ton of stress on one's psyche, leading to poor decision-making and control in these circumstances.

For instance, as a parent, when you observe your children arguing and fighting with each other, it is important to hold your composure. You must approach the situation rationally and carefully analyze both of their perspectives and perhaps have them compromise to move forward from the situation. It is easy to lose one's cool or temper during these situations, which could lead to scolding children or taking away their games or toys as a means of punishment. While punishment plays a role in learning, there are always more receptive ways of teaching your children. By staying calm and considering the various factors surrounding their scuffle, you can come up with the appropriate decision for that situation instead of making a rash one with potentially irreparable consequences for you and the children (e.g., they stop listening to you after several episodes of punishment).

By induction, it is, of course, important for a leader to hold composure as well because he or she is required to make time-sensitive decisions at times with vastly different outcomes depending on the decision. For instance, if you are a leader of an organization raising funds to hold an event, you need to be mentally prepared for the worst. If it turns out that sponsor organizations fail to fund your organization or retract on their promise, one must maintain composure to find solutions to this seeming conundrum. Maybe there was a misunderstanding, so you can recontact these organizations. Or perhaps there are a few organizations you have not considered for funding your event. If a leader panics in this situation, he or she may develop and encapsulate a fear of failure and make hasty decisions with poor outcomes (e.g., making last-minute cuts on food costs or renegotiating a contract with a keynote speaker, paying him or her less for the talk).

From May 1988, I recall an eighty-six-year-old male patient who was brought to the ER by his six sons. He belonged to a royal family in Saudi Arabia and was visiting the Al-Midhnab area. I was called to the ER to examine that patient. When I walked into his room, the patient was unconscious. One of his sons told me that the patient was having rectal bleeding onset two hours prior to coming to the ER. When I tried asking other questions relevant to his medical history, his son told me, "You are the doctor. Tell us what is going on with him."

When he told me this, I held my composure and confidently told them, "No problem. I will evaluate and diagnose your father's condition." As a doctor, you need as much information as possible about a patient's health prior to making a firm diagnosis and coming up with a corresponding treatment plan. I noticed yellow discoloration of the patient's skin and sclera, both of which are indicative of jaundice, a liver disease. I quickly performed my clinical examination, in which I palpated his abdomen and noted that the liver was enlarged and noted a cecum mass in the right iliac fossa with free fluid in the abdomen.

I decided to perform a rectal exam to exclude any local pathology, which showed occult and fresh blood. My clinical diagnosis was carcinoma of cecum with metastasis in liver and peritoneum, which I wrote in the patient's chart and in the radiology request form. I advised routine lab tests and called the radiologist on call to do an urgent abdominal ultrasound and a barium enema to see any gastrointestinal obstruction to further evaluate the cecum to exclude malignancy. The radiologist noted that the barium dye was not going up the patient's intestine in the barium enema, indicating that there was a mass, and the ultrasound showed metastasis in the liver and peritoneum. After two hours of labs, the radiologist brought his test reports; and he highly appreciated my clinical diagnosis, which was correct. He told me that he loved working with me because I ordered minimally relevant labs and radiological tests.

After all that testing, the patient's sons surrounded me and asked, "What is his diagnosis?"

I informed them, "I am sorry. Your father is suffering from a carcinoma of cecum with metastasis in liver and peritoneum."

They began smiling and were satisfied, telling me, "You are the best doctor. We were actually aware of our father's diagnosis, but we did not tell you that because we wanted to test your judgment. Despite that, you correctly diagnosed him. Good job." One of his sons told me that their father was getting treatment for his cancer at the King Fahad Hospital in Riyadh, so they asked if we could transport him there. I obtained permission from the hospital director, prepared a medical report, and arranged transportation via a medical helicopter so that he may get his treatment.

I felt that they came to the ER simply to test me. However, I learned a very valuable lesson in maintaining my composure when dealing with this clinical case and that taught me how to better manage my future patients.

Open-Mindedness

Open-mindedness is the ability to accept novel ideas and thoughts into one's repository of thoughts. It entails "thinking outside of the box," considering unique, uncommon solutions to common and uncommon problems we face on a daily basis. An important aspect of open-mindedness, I believe, is to approach difficult scenarios with an open mind, or a *tabula rasa*—to look at them from a different angle or perspective one would not normally consider. By making decisions under this umbrella of open-mindedness, you have to be willing to take a risk, regardless of whether this risk entails a low-reward yield in the outcome, embarrassment, or failure.

To illustrate the value of open-mindedness, let's do a thought experiment. Think of something you do on a daily basis to which you don't give a second thought. Perhaps this is something you are doing while reading the words on this page. For instance, one activity that many of us engage in throughout the day is walking. When we walk, whether it is inside our homes, at work, or while observing nature, we almost never pay attention to the fact that we are walking. It never occurs to us that we may be walking incorrectly. What I mean by this is that we may have a bad posture when walking or have an unsteady gait. Now I am sure that if we go to a doctor or some other professional, he or she can assess the way we walk and give us advice or consultation as to how we can improve our walking and prevent any health issues down the road. However, to even get to this level of thinking, you have to approach the activities you do from the perspective that you have no idea or experience in doing that activity. With walking, you need to take a few steps back and consider: "Am I walking properly? Do I have a steady gait? Do I have any leg or lower back pain?" These questions may seem silly, but they all necessitate being open-minded to even ask oneself these questions. Getting the answers to these questions will allow us to uncover new information or a novel method of doing a particular activity. This unleashes new ways of thinking and will expand one's repository of knowledge.

In July 1992, I recall meeting a twenty-one-year-old male Saudi patient who came to my clinic complaining of on-and-off dizziness, palpitations, and shortness of breath onset the last two years, stating that these symptoms only occurred upon physical exertion or strenuous activities. His last episode was the evening prior when he was playing soccer and suddenly experienced dizziness, palpitation, and shortness of breath. He did not take any medications at the time. To alleviate his symptoms, he sat down and relaxed for twenty to thirty minutes, at the end of which he returned back to baseline. He informed me that he was seen by several physicians from other hospitals, who all informed him that he was suffering from anxiety and told him to not be overly concerned about his symptoms.

While having respect for the other providers' unanimous diagnosis, I still wanted to go through a physical examination and assessment to approach this situation from a new light and to apply a new pair of eyes to his symptoms. After my physical examination, I did not note any unusual clinical signs or symptoms, such as palpitations or tachycardia, which would have been indicative of some anxiety. The next thing that came to my mind was that he may have had a defect in his cardiac conductive tissues, which generate his heartbeat and are triggered during exercise. I thought that there may have been some accessory pathway that got triggered when he played soccer. I remembered a similar case at Karachi Jinnah Postgraduate Medical Center when I was doing my three-month course in advanced cardiology under Professor Shaukat Syed. In light of this, I asked my nurse to perform an EKG on him in the resting position, which showed normal sinuses and rhythm.

At that point, I could have done what most physicians would have done, which would either have been to closely monitor his symptoms and ask him to come back for a follow-up or refer him for a cardiologist consult. However, at that moment, I started considering the more rare possibilities. Based on my clinical intuition, I had this epiphany that he may have Wolff-Parkinson-White syndrome, which manifests in patients through shortness of breath, rapid pulse, and dizziness. Therefore, under my supervision while the patient still had EKG leads attached to his chest, I requested him to run for three to five minutes in front of my clinic area. After he came back, he appeared winded and started complaining of palpitations but no chest pain. I immediately had the nurse redo the EKG, which showed a delta wave in the precordial lead V1, which was a diagnostic for Wolff-Parkinson-White (WPW) syndrome. A delta wave is a slurred upstroke in the QRS complex and has a short PR interval. This syndrome is usually caused by the presence of an abnormal accessory electrical pathway between the atria and ventricles called the Bundle of Kent. This abnormal pathway electrically signals the heart to contract prematurely, which leads to supraventricular tachycardia. WPW syndrome is a very rare condition that affects between 0.1 and 0.3 percent in the population. My diagnosis was confirmed as WPW syndrome type A because of a positive R wave that was seen in V1 lead. I called a renowned cardiac electrophysiologist at the King Fahad Hospital in Rayed to present this case. I reported my physical examination, EKG findings, and ultimate diagnosis of WPW syndrome type A to the cardiac electrophysiologist and ultimately referred that patient to him.

Meanwhile, I explained to the patient that the condition had a cure, which entailed the destruction of the abnormal electrical pathway by radiofrequency through catheter ablation. After four weeks, the cardiac electrophysiologist forwarded a report regarding the progress of this procedure with a final diagnosis of WPW syndrome type A. He was really surprised that I was able to come to the conclusion that the patient had WPW syndrome. In his five years of practice, he had not seen a single case of WPW syndrome. He appreciated and commended my clinical intuition for obtaining a prompt diagnosis and referral for treatment.

Similarly, in April 1993, I examined a twenty-three-year-old female patient who was eight months pregnant. She was referred from the ob-gyn clinic for evaluation of her shortness of breath and palpitation, which she noticed very recently. I was compelled to believe that the patient may have WPW syndrome based upon my clinical intuition and the fact that I had seen a similar case less than a year ago.

Like with the male patient with WPW in July 1992, I had the nurse perform a resting EKG on the patient, which showed normal sinuses and rhythm. However, the follow-up EKG after the patient did some brisk walking showed negative delta waves in V1 consistent to WPW syndrome type B due to excitation of right atrioventricular connections. I chose to wait until her baby was delivered before I referred her to the cardiac electrophysiologist because the catheter ablation could lead to unintended consequences for her unborn child. In July 1993, a couple of months after delivering her baby, the patient had the procedure done by the electrophysiologist and has recovered fully.

These two cases demonstrated a degree of open-mindedness to correctly diagnose the cause of their symptoms. I could have followed standard protocol for these patients and had them referred to cardiology immediately after their resting EKGs were normal. Instead, I chose to take the path less traveled and see if my clinical intuition had any weight to it. In both instances, I took a novel approach at the time to make my assessment, providing patients with the immediate relief that comes from understanding the unknown.

Below is a published article that I wrote in 2016. It demonstrates the value of clinical intuition and having an open-minded approach when deciding what treatment route I want to go down.

This article, "The Value of Clinical Intuition: Kids Also Get Drug Side Effects," was published in *Inner Circle Executive* (ICE) 3 Autumn 16-W3, December 2016 edition.

> In my own career, clinical intuition has proven useful. From 1988–1993, I was an internist and pulmonologist at Al Midhnab General Hospital Saudi Arabia.
>
> One warm night in July 1988, we had a 6-year-old child present to the ER with suspected meningitis. The chief pediatrician who was handling this case was explaining the situation to the father, when I happened to walk by while rounding my patients. I overhead him say that they would get a lumbar puncture done and admit the child. To this day, I can't tell you what compelled me to take a look. But I did. And I saw the child with the head tilted toward the right side: a right dystonia. Perhaps it was something in the child's expression, the way he looked, or his demeanor. Or maybe it was that the child wasn't overtly expressing infectious symptoms like fever, headache, etc. All I knew was that my instincts were telling me that we weren't dealing with meningitis. My mind was gravitating toward a medication side effect that I had seen countless times in my training. The anxious expression of the child was all the motivation I needed to step in and confirm the possibility my mind had hatched.

Getting permission from the pediatrician to evaluate the patient, I elicited a history from the father, focusing particularly on medications. I learned that the child had vomiting bouts a couple days ago and was given metoclopramide. Afterwards, he began presenting with right neck dystonia later that day. This was a common side effect of the medication, which I knew from my past experience working in psychiatric wards. My diagnosis clinched, I asked the nurse to prepare a valium injection. Once the injection was given, the child's head began to rotate slowly back to normal like clockwork. Everyone was stunned. The father could not stop shaking my hand, and the pediatrician was in awe. The child, sullen-faced earlier, was overjoyed. This may seem like a non-replicable, isolated incident. However, I assure you that many physicians have had similar experiences. Now the question is how do we teach this kind of skill?

A possible answer is that it comes from exposure to many permutations of clinical cases and symptoms with the goal of treating the patient holistically; a conclusion supported by Brokensha's review from 2002. Furthermore, I will add that the art of the physical diagnosis is an essential part of the intuition and is central to developing strong observation skills. During my training, we took an exam where a standardized patient was evaluated in 15 minutes, where the student had to rely on his observation skill, palpatory, and physical exam skills to come to a diagnosis. In Pakistan, with the lack of resources in many clinics, it was imperative to master this skill. With the passage of the Affordable Care Act, I see a similar discussion taking place in the United States.

A class focusing on developing clinical intuition into our medical curriculum can be a starting point. Maybe experienced physicians can keep a journal of interesting cases relying on their clinical intuition and then pass it on. Clinical intuition is still a valuable skill in modern health care and is both a celebration of our roots as healers and a lantern to the future of our profession.

References: Brokensha, Glyn. (2002). "Clinical Intuition: More than Rational?" *Australian Prescriber*, January, Issue 25, 14–15.

By maintaining open-mindedness, readers can start making unique decisions in their life as a part of understanding the world around them in a way they may have never considered otherwise. For me, open-mindedness contributes to my happiness and gives me great pleasure and diversity in the activities I do and in my thought process.

Courage

Courage is a quality or mental state that allows one to face difficult challenges and conquer their fears with confidence. Courage is also necessary in making difficult decisions, especially those in opposition. Making the right decision isn't always easy or popular, which is why a leader needs to have the courage to make tough decisions when necessary. Whether standing up for important principles, facing down enemies, or charting a new and difficult course, a leader will always be defined by his or her courage or lack thereof.

At the Baqai Hospital in Karachi, Pakistan, in June 1994, I remember a case of a forty-year-old man presenting to the clinic with a history of recent weight loss, fever, and night sweats. He was very overt about his weight loss. He was being assessed by a different provider at our clinic, and I was overhearing her assessment and plan from afar as I managed my own patient. At some point, I glanced over and noticed the emaciated man. His image is still burned into my memory. I noticed there was no eye contact between the patient and the other physician, who was taking notes on his patient chart. She told the patient that she would give him analgesics and some vitamins. As she said that, I noticed very conspicuous enlarged lymph nodes to his neck from about twenty-five feet away. He was also sweating and actively appeared have a fever. My clinical intuition told me that the patient was suffering from some form of a lymphoma and needed to be admitted for a lymph node biopsy to distinguish Hodgkin's lymphoma from non-Hodgkin's lymphoma. The presence of Reed-Sternberg cells would indicate Hodgkin's lymphoma. Excusing myself from my patient, I decided to go to the attending physician, and I politely asked her to allow me to see the patient in order to confirm my diagnosis and hospitalize the patient. Permission was granted, and I examined this patient and confirmed Hodgkin's lymphoma diagnosis through the biopsy and other testing. Both the patient and physician were thankful to me for this intervention.

Now I am sure many of us have found ourselves in similar situations where someone is suffering or is having a problem being managed by another person or even unmanaged. In these situations, to maintain good relations, we usually become bystanders and try not to interfere with that individual and those tending to that individual's issues. For instance, in the work environment, you may see a coworker having an issue with his or her computer and be unwilling to help because it is technically not your responsibility. However, it requires a certain degree of courage and boldness to directly tackle the issue despite what your coworker might think. The person could indeed thank you for your kindness, but he or she could also take it negatively, as you helping could make him or her feel inferior or incompetent.

As a physician, I could have permanently damaged my relationship with the attending physician tending to her patient by interfering and perhaps making her feel incompetent, but it was the right thing to do because of the patient's treatment. And, therefore, his quality of life superseded the mutual friendly relationship between us.

Compassion

An important portion of leadership is the ability to motivate people and demonstrate compassion and understanding over their unique backgrounds. In order to motivate people, one must listen, maintain eye contact, and show genuine concern. Having compassion truly elevates one to the highest level of morality because it necessarily entails putting oneself in the shoes of others and requires one, at the very least, to try to understand the human experience from that individual's perspective. Even if I will perhaps never be able to fully experience what the other is feeling due to socioeconomic, religious, ethnic, and racial factors in addition to his or her unique personal upbringings, the intent to understand the other and to do whatever one can with a given power is perhaps more important than being successful in showing sympathy or empathy for that individual.

While I was practicing at the Karachi Psychiatric Hospital in 1987, I remember a twenty-four-year-old man who came to me with sex anxiety and a fear of failure on the first night of marriage. His marriage ceremony was actually scheduled the same day within the next four to five hours. He was anxious and worried that he couldn't perform intercourse effectively after his wedding. It was difficult for any physician to treat his anxiety in a few hours. Immediately, I accepted this challenge to treat him despite not having gone through marriage at the time.

The first thing that came to my mind was how to successfully reduce his fear. I needed to draw out his inner confidence and consult him effectively. I started by taking a meticulous patient history and physical examination to rule out a pathophysiological cause relating to perhaps a sex organ defect. After ruling out any organ-related issues, I was sure he was suffering from sex anxiety. I put myself in his shoes and firmly reassured him that he had no sexual abnormality or a disorder of medical etiology. I spent an hour consulting him, during which he intently paid attention to what I had to say. I reciprocated with keen eye contact to demonstrate my empathy for him. During that span, we started to develop a strong bond with each other. After consulting him, I noticed the anxiety creep off his face, which was now illuminated with hope. I gave him some tips pertaining to relaxation therapy in concomitance with providing him with a low dose of an antianxiolytic, which I encouraged him to take an hour prior to engaging in sex if necessary. I could tell that a medication was not a cure-all for his anxiety, but I prescribed it to him so that he might attain a state of mental peace. I asked him to follow up with me the following day.

The next day, he arrived and was beaming about his success during the last night. He commended me for the time I spent the day prior reassuring him because it had truly boosted his confidence and morale. However, to ensure and differentiate the success from medication versus my consult, I gave him a one-week follow-up and advised him to use the medication when necessary. After one week, the patient was perfectly normal, and he even informed me that he did not use medicine except on his wedding night. Whether the patient is treated with medications or not is beside the point. Instead, it is important to show compassion and empathy for patients by listening to what they have to say and not dismissing any of their medical issues.

Optimism

Optimism is the state of being where one always considers the most positive outcomes of any particular situation despite there being room for equally possible negative outcomes. A classic example to illustrate optimism is that of a glass of water. Imagine someone pouring water into a glass to about the halfway mark. Now, when you look at the glass, what do you see? Do you see the glass half full with water or rather half empty? If you look at the glass half empty, then you are very likely a pessimist—a negative thinker—and likely think of the worst outcomes of any particular scenario. On the other hand, if you see the glass as half full, you are more than likely an optimist—a positive thinker, considering the best outcomes when confronted with dilemmas. For leaders, while it is important to consider both sides of the coin, it is far more crucial to be optimistic when making decisions.

In the same vein, optimism also entails having a lack of fear of failure and accepting arduous challenges. If a leader is pessimistic, he or she will likely make the incorrect, least optimal decision or make no decision at all. However, a true leader—a natural-born leader—thinks positively, lacks a fear of failure, and hence makes high-risk, high-reward decisions. He or she is ready to accept the consequences of making the wrong decisions and willing to learn from these mistakes.

As a doctor and a leader, a fighting spirit always gives you good results. In November 1989, I received a call from a nurse who informed me that a patient of mine, a sixty-five-year-old female, suddenly went into cardiac arrest with there being a straight line on the EKG monitor. I was on call at the time and in my apartment located inside the hospital campus. It was a five- to seven-minute walk, but knowing the urgency of the situation, I remember I did a combination of brisk walking and running to get to the patient on time. Generally, after approximately ten minutes of cardiac arrest, patients are at the point of no return; and if they do return, they will be in vegetative state. Very rarely do patients resuscitated after ten minutes return to their baseline health.

When I arrived, ten to fifteen minutes had already passed with cardiac arrest. I immediately started cardiopulmonary resuscitation by using a cardiac defibrillator and other supportive treatment. After another ten to fifteen minutes of persistence, some cardiac rhythm returned, and she started breathing through a bag valve mask. At that point, we prepared her for transfer to the ICU. The resident doctor only then arrived during the transfer of the patient to the ICU because he was busy dealing with another emergency case in the ER. During the next thirty minutes, I managed her arrhythmia back to normal sinuses and rhythm by giving antiarrhythmic medication, and she regained consciousness. That meant that the brain was not affected during that prolonged period of cardiac arrest. Later on, I was following up with that patient to see any onset of renal failure. I was surprised to find that both the brain and kidneys were functioning normally. During the monitoring period, the patient was fully conscious, oriented, and did not have any residual symptoms of cardiac arrest.

In all, she was under cardiac arrest for thirty minutes before partial resuscitation. It was always my habit to work for a longer period of time to save the life of a patient as a true fighter. I could have easily given up hope arriving to the hospital ten to fifteen minutes after her cardiac arrest began, knowing patients in her position were at the point of no return, but I persevered and continued to fight. She may have been 99 percent dead, but there was a 1 percent chance that I could save her. I took that chance. To this day, that patient case goes down as one of my most memorable and sentimental ones. To this day, it brings tears to my eyes that I was able to resuscitate her and return her to baseline without any complications.

Chapter 7

Leadership Intuition

What Is Leadership Intuition?

Prior to working in Saudi Arabia, I did not have what I call leadership intuition because I never got the chance to play a leadership role. I remember that it was a tough time for me early during my tenure in Saudi Arabia because the hospital administrator wanted me to accept the position of the chief of medicine. He praised my insightfulness, self-confidence, and composure in the medical field. I give him immense credit due to the intense scrutiny he placed me under because that gave me the opportunity to hold my first leadership position as the chief of medicine, which ultimately served as the stepping-stone in developing my leadership intuition. It has allowed me to combat complex issues in a timely manner even until today.

Examples of Leadership Intuition at JBVAMC 2000–15

I have used my leadership intuition working at JBVAMC in Chicago, Illinois, where I started working in 2000 and am still working there to this day as a research compliance officer. Prior to working at the VA, I did not have any experience working in research administration. However, my education and background working as a medical doctor and holding leadership positions, such as hospital administrator and chief of medicine, in the past were the source of my insight and self-confidence when entering this new field. I quickly picked up the importance of and how to manage an entire research administration, including research compliance, and all aspects of clinical research on human subjects and laboratory research on animal subjects in the research and development (R&D) department at JBVAMC.

Challenging Task 1: AAALAC

I worked to prepare the JBVAMC animal care accreditation program on November 16, 2002, for the AAALAC (Association for Assessment of Laboratory Animal Care International Accreditation) Audit. Simply put, the audit entailed meticulously looking through and reviewing thousands of pages of paperwork pertaining to active research studies. This required much persistence and intrinsic motivation, as you may imagine, in reviewing all those pages. By having a positive mind-set and target in mind, I was able to successfully complete the audit on time, and it was met with great success. The audit received three years of accreditation and appreciation from auditors for maintaining a high standard relating to animal care in research projects. The investigators' research files from various committees, training documentations, and VA federal grant were all approved for on-site at JBVAMC and off-site researchers from the University of Illinois at Chicago and Northwestern University. It was my first accreditation audit, and it was very successful, being highly appreciated by the hospital director and various committee members.

Challenging Task 2: FDA Audit

I remember on December 15, 2002, at about 4:00 p.m., the associate chief of staff for the R&D department had received a call from the Food and Drug Administration (FDA). They called to inform us that they would send an auditor on December 17, 2002, to review investigational drug and medical device protocols, documentation of FDA special forms to conduct FDA-approved research on human subjects, and research investigators' training documentations, in addition to other things. Immediately, my boss called me. I went to his office, and I noticed that he was not physically or mentally prepared for this FDA audit, having only two days to prepare. I assured him that I would be ready for this audit even if it were tomorrow. My boss was surprised, and I told him, "Please don't worry; I will take responsibility and have them come tomorrow."

I asked him for the auditor's name and telephone number. I proceed to call her, and I requested that she come the next morning, December 16, 2002, at 8:00 a.m. The auditor was also astonished and agreed to come the next day. At that time, I had already prepared around thirty active research protocols for her to review the next morning. The following morning, the FDA auditor did not find any deficiencies and approved continuation of the research studies.

That experience exemplified my composure and insightfulness. I did not crumble under the impromptu audit and even assured my boss that I would be prepared for it despite the circumstances. It was my mentality from the beginning to be ready for any surprise audit. That readiness contributed to a successful audit.

Challenging Task 3: JCAHO Audit

On January 18, 2005, I completed the JCAHO (Joint Commission Accreditation Hospital Organization) audit related to the Human Research Protection Program (HRPP). The audit required composure on my end because it was a surprise audit. Having gone through similar cases in the past, I was better prepared to handle ones like that. Ultimately, that audit received a perfect score.

Challenging Task 4: Office of Research Oversight (ORO), Midwest Region Site Visit

I was working as a research coordinator for the HRPP at the time when the Office of Research Oversight (ORO) Midwest Region site visit team planned a visit from March 21 to 24, 2005, in February 2005. Over the span of a month, leading up to the site visit, I had to manage over 150 research protocols across JBVAMC and University of Illinois at Chicago, requiring much diligence and attention to detail, and this was in addition to doing my usual job description. It was a very stressful time, but my compassion and focus on getting the task done pushed me past the finish line. The ORO could not believe that a single individual could accomplish such a high quantity of tasks with high quality as well. The ORO team also commended me for developing and maintaining one of the best HRPP programs in the Midwest Region.

Challenging Task 5: The National Committee for Quality Assurance (NCQA) Accreditation Audit for the Human Research Protection Program (HRPP)

This was perhaps one of the biggest projects I performed during my time at VA. In June 2005, I remember my boss called me and requested that I prepare JBVAMC Chicago, Illinois, Research and Development Department for the National Committee for Quality Assurance (NCQA) accreditation audit for the HRPP on October 17, 2005. I accepted that challenge alone. Four to five months remained for that audit. In addition to those responsibilities, I was overseeing the R&D committee, research safety subcommittee, research space subcommittee, and the annual board of directors' meeting (nonprofit corporation), preparing policies and procedures and developing performance improvement plans while organizing research seminars and safety training meetings. I was doing all that work during my regular job hours and moreover stayed at work every day from 4:00 p.m. to 10:00 p.m. without additional compensation to prepare for the NCQA audit.

I prepared sixteen new standard operating procedures (SOPs) and revised eight current SOPs to meet the audit requirement. I further ensured training for all research investigators and their team members and asked special permission to go to the JBVAMC pharmacy to ensure they were dispensing investigational drugs and medical devices according to the IRB-approved protocols and the VA pharmacy regulations in dispensing and storing medicine, respectively. I worked two weeks in the pharmacy prior to that audit, making sure that the pharmacy was following protocol. For instance, the pharmacy needed to ensure that medicines were refrigerated at their desired temperatures to avoid the deterioration of these medications.

On audit day at the pharmacy, I asked the NCQA auditor if I could stay in the pharmacy so that they may ask questions if and when appropriate. I settled on doing this because at that time, the research pharmacist was new. Permission was granted. During the audit, the auditor was asking many questions and required documentation to meet the accreditation requirements. I was answering all her questions and concerns. At one point, she asked about the expiration date of one of the drugs being tested by a VA collaborative research team. The pharmacist was unaware of the situation entirely. I interjected and provided her with the answer. "The NCQA audit regulation indicates that the VA central office at Washington, DC, will keep the expiration date of medicine used by VA collaborative research studies." Luckily, I had the insight to provide her with this answer.

The auditor asked me, "Where is this regulation written?" I had a regulatory file with me, and I showed it to her. The auditor was surprised and asked me, "How do you remember this detail?"

I responded to her, "It's because I worked independently for this preparation. I remember each and every detail about this audit."

By doing all those preparations, I met 102 standards and 257 elements and factors to score a perfect 100 percent compliance at first attempt. It was one of the greatest honors for the JBVAMC to achieve the highest possible score in the HRPP out of 116 veteran affair hospitals throughout the USA. The R&D department was proud of my efforts to achieve that seemingly impossible goal and save the facility several thousand dollars of revenue in potential consultation fees.

All the regulatory agencies were amazed with my knowledge, excellent job performance, and total command of federal and state regulations. They could not believe that one person could complete all that work with such high standards.

In view of my excellent service, which far exceeded my job description, the R&D department nominated me for the 2006 Chicago Federal Employee of the Year Award, which I won in the category of program specialist. These achievements gave me more confidence and internal happiness.

Challenging Task 6: Formation of Single IRB

The Jesse Brown VA Medical Center Human Research Protection Program was a complex program, dealing with two academic affiliates in which it managed five Northwestern University (NU) IRB panels and three University of Illinois at Chicago (UIC) IRB boards. I worked together with the directors of OPRS at UIC and ACOS R&D to make a single UIC IRB no. 4 to deal with all research projects from JBVAMC, NU, and UIC, allowing these projects to be reviewed under one IRB. That displayed my open-mindedness and ability to work with others in making cognizant decisions. The IRB began operating in July 2008.

Now, in June 2015, the JBVAMC has its own IRB instead of going to the UIC IRB no. 4, which have since been transferred to JBVAMC.

Challenging Task 7: AAHRPP Audit

In 2007–8, another HRPP accreditation audit was required because the previous accreditation audit had met the end of its three-year approval period. Therefore, all VA research programs were required to go to a new agency for accreditation. It was the Association for the Accreditation of Human Research Protection Program (AAHRPP) accreditation audit, which was scheduled September 26–28, 2007, with our two affiliates—UIC and NU.

Again, my boss called me and requested that I prepare the JBVAMC for a new research program accreditation. I was ready to accept the challenge as I had before in 2005. I spent additional hours at work to accomplish this job in two months.

The AAHRPP accreditation required fulfilling documentation and implementation of five domains, twenty standards, and seventy-seven elements. I started an element-by-element review of the HRPP using a gap analysis and generating new policies and procedures to modify it in order to meet the AAHRPP standards.

I completed the AAHRPP application process, which entailed preparing a 2,951-page report in two months (April/May 2007) along with my day-to-day operations. This work was highly appreciated by the associate chief of staff of the R&D and medical center director and directors at NU and UIC.

Reaccreditation was required by AAHRPP auditors every three years after getting approval in 2008. From October 24–25, 2011, there was another reaccreditation audit. I served as the leader of the R&D team, and we prepared for the audit together. After preparing several audits on my own, I had obtained the confidence and insight to convey my knowledge to others in order to optimize the process. We did it as a team and obtained accreditation for five years in March 2012.

In all those projects, my complex background and education helped me to understand the goals of the various research programs. I used my NBL abilities in managing two academic affiliates of the JBVAMC, UIC and NU, with a high degree of efficiency. I was reviewing, auditing, and preparing audit reports with remedial action plans or noncompliance-related findings to the various research oversight committees, such as the ORO in Washington, DC.

I demonstrated high levels of focus and determination when it came to be completing an assignment or task. I had created and maintained excellent lines of communication with local, regional, and national VA services, UIC IRB, and the UIC protocol office. These lines of communication enabled me to find innovative solutions to complex problems. If there was a problem, I recognized it and looked for a solution even if it was not my responsibility.

I am currently maintaining a high quality of state-of-the-art activities to create a constructive environment to help researchers interact so that new programs and collaboration can be developed. I am also providing one-on-one education and training to all research community members according to recent changes in the federal regulations to achieve maximum compliance with VA regulations to conduct research at JBVAMC. For the last three years, I have been the editor for the *R&D Research Newsletter*, in which I introduced the recognition of "Research of the Month," which showed and continues to show researchers' appreciation for their hard work.

Discussion on Leadership Intuition

Throughout my career, I found myself working under time-sensitive, high-risk, and high-pressure situations, which allowed me to uncover and develop my NBL qualities. Today, I am glad to write about my findings as an NBL, and I hope it will be interesting and exciting for readers.

I began thinking like an NBL from a young age. I was a very obedient and disciplined child at home. I was ready to help everyone even though I was very busy in my studies. I would balance my time throughout the day to find the time to help others. I would never say no. Helping others gave me this unique internal satisfaction. After becoming a doctor in 1980, I would willingly provide free medical treatment to many in my own neighborhood, going to their homes to inject IV fluids or even buying them medicine if they could not afford it.

I feel that leaders nowadays are susceptible to burning out at the workplace. My philosophy is that if there is an expectation that is not realistically achievable and ultimately is unachieved, it will lead to burnout. I approach my work life in a very easygoing fashion. The salary I earn has to simply be good enough to meet basic life necessities and to provide for my family. In my thirty-six years of professional work, I received several job offers from various third world countries or even from many United States organizations, but I declined the vast majority of them because I didn't choose to chase higher-salary occupations; that was not my priority. I sacrificed these offers for my kids so that they could get a better education and one day become professionals. My only preference was a workplace where I could have peace of mind and would have the goal to work with what I had to enhance the reputation of that work organization.

The NBL avoids these burnouts by his or her positive and strong mentality. The NBL is target-oriented, focused, self-confident, and intrinsically motivated to accomplish tasks. These leaders enter a certain uninterruptible state of flow when working on their tasks because they are fully absorbed in their work, not paying attention to any factors external to those tasks. Once they return from this state, they feel a sense of pleasure, which invigorates them, allowing them to use their unique skill set to tackle further projects.

The fear of failure also fuels these burnouts. These kinds of leaders treat failure as an almost necessary evil to achieve success. Don't view it as that. Think of it as a teacher—a hard teacher and one that does very little encouragement but, in the end, is always looking out for your best interest.

Personally, I think leadership is a mind-set, and it boils down to being able to take actions that are in line with one's principles and what's important to you. Everyone seeks happiness. Power, money, beauty, and health will not lead to happiness on their own. They alone don't lead to happiness. Many people in these categories are often afflicted with anxiety and boredom. Ask yourself whether these things can truly lead to your happiness. The following is my advice for happiness.

Since childhood, I never ran after money or tried to use my accomplishments as a symbol to society that I had arrived. I am happy with what I have and satisfied with that, but I continue my struggle to improve each aspect of my life. I developed positive thinking toward life, and I am grateful for the fortunes and blessings in my life. I have no frustration or anxiety. Now happiness is in my nature because I have daily goals for myself, and after achieving a target, I feel happy that I have accomplished something on that day, and the day was not wasted.

I always set targets for myself one week in advance as it relates to my job, home, and family needs. As I write this chapter, my target for the day was to get my car checked out, cook food, and then spend the day completing my book. After finishing cooking, for instance, I tell my heart that I have completed this task, which gives me happiness and ignites my desire to start the next task of the day. This type of feeling will not come automatically; you must be intrinsically motivated to achieve this state.

Break your day down into tiny bits. Break it into manageable pieces. Even things as mundane as taking the trash out, cleaning your room, and really anything else can be a source of joy and fulfillment.

This also happens because I am compassionate about my work. The state of flow I mentioned earlier leads to optimal experiences. On rare occasions, people feel a sense of exhilaration, a deep sense of enjoyment, when going through a certain experience. It becomes a landmark in one's life. With the right mentality, this optimal experience can be obtained up to several times a day. By entering this state of flow over the course of a long period of time, it adds up to give a sense of happiness. Reaching the optimal experience can be exercised by anyone, regardless of age, gender, or cultural and religious backgrounds.

I learned and gained huge confidence on how to develop abilities related to risk management as a hospital administrator in Saudi Arabia under MOH without any additional salary. Those were my glory days, when I enjoyed the authority, treating patients, dealing with nurses and hospital staff, including doctors and patient-relation department, Saudi and non-Saudi staffs, and doing justice with all hospital employees. I was conducting five high-level meetings as a head chair while dealing with day-to-day hospital activities. I remembered that I never thought of my occupation as a *job*, but I treated it broadly as *work*. I was working toward a vision for the sake of the hospital management and patients out of internal pride and happiness.

That was very important to me. I was flexible and would do anything in order to maintain that vision. That has been a constant theme for me since I completed my medical residency in Pakistan to working in the Al-Midhnab Hospital to now working at Jesse Brown VA Medical Center in the United States.

Harnessing the State of Flow

Challenging Task
or Project

Apply Skill(s) 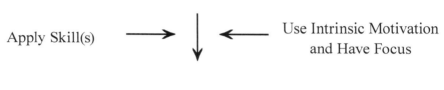 Use Intrinsic Motivation
and Have Focus

State of Flow

Optimal Experience

Happiness and
Internal Pleasure

Chapter 8

Conclusion and Self-Assessment Tool to Identify NBL Abilities

According to my fifty years of continuous self-assessment, observation, and experience, I reached the following conclusions.

Perhaps many readers of this book did not agree with me, but I am sure that if readers went through various hardships and achieved great success, then they will be able to sympathize with my lifelong struggle to find something good for the future generation and the betterment of their lives. My thought is that if our leaders all over the world are sincere in their decision-making and seek genuine understanding, they will be successful. They will find the real cause of worldwide issues.

This book is as much an exploration of NBL as it is an autobiography. I implemented various principles and applied them through the various projects that I performed while living in Pakistan, Saudi Arabia, and the USA. Furthermore, I have outlined a performance-based tool that takes into account many of the qualities essential to NBL. The tool utilizes an easy scoring system that will assist one in determining his or her leadership qualities. By using this tool, people can discover if they have the qualities to determine if they can become powerful leaders in their respective organizations.

NBL abilities will start grooming from childhood.

In my childhood, I remember that my parents demonstrated various daily activities at home, and I learned a set of qualities through scrupulous observation: obedience to elders, respect, honesty, hard work, self-sacrifices, discipline at home and school, and determination. For me, these values gradually developed, and after reaching success in the activities I engaged in at a young age, I obtained self-confidence, which only bolstered over time. I think this kind of a confidence from childhood is what we need to be equipped with the tools to become an NBL down the line.

I believe everyone is born with equal abilities. However, the environment where a child is raised, his parents, and education help in developing and finding NBL abilities. For example, storytelling is also very insightful to kids as they develop their imaginations and sharpen their memories by engaging themselves in these stories. It will only develop once the kids find themselves interested in good, moral, thoughtful stories. I have my example of telling stories to my two kids almost daily for ten years. I would also test my children on their math skills from a young age, from basic addition and subtraction to multiplication. My youngest son has told me, "Those math questions you used to ask me daily really helped develop a foundation in my basic math skills, which has allowed me to stay ahead of the curve and built confidence in me when confronted with new math concepts at school, knowing I had this solid foundation in my arsenal."

Both my kids are now studying in a medical school to become doctors to serve humanity, not just make money. In my personal experience, I had the same mentality. My wish is that they continue my legacy.

As a child, I started by helping in the kitchen, with laundry, and with cleaning the home, which helped me perfect my time-management and organization skills. I developed these two NBL abilities from a young age, and these proved to be very helpful throughout my career.

As an internist and pulmonologist, I learned the art of listening to my patients' concerns and sacrificing my time and money for my patients—even buying medicine out of my own pocket for poor patients by going two miles away to the pharmacy to purchase the medicine. My philosophy was to become a doctor for serving humanity. My recommendation is if someone wants to earn money, please don't pursue the medical field. There is no need to run behind money, putting oneself under immense frustration, anxiety, loss of sleep, irritability, anger, and dissatisfaction with the amount earned. This will only result in ruining your family life and damaging your children's mentality concerning money.

NBLs have a cohort of abilities and qualities that make them great role models and help them lead others. They are self-directed and often establish norms. They are charismatic with the ability to inspire and motivate others to accomplish their goals with positive outcomes. The NBL has an intuition, which is difficult to describe, but personally, I think it entails having an art of observation, integrating nonverbal information during high-risk, time-sensitive situations. I myself have obtained clinical and nonclinical intuition through my career using this approach, and I have been able to make several crucial decisions thereof. Strong leaders are the ones that the company and other employees can trust because of their values, integrity, and morals.

The NBL maintains clear, consistent communication with his or her employees. Constant communication makes employees understand the company's vision, giving them an assurance that they are working toward the desired goals. Confidence is essential for strong leadership when the future of the company, corporation, or organization is at stake.

Natural-born leaders have solutions to each and every problem in this world, whether political or nonpolitical. These leaders must do so to find these solutions while maintaining a high degree of integrity to make the right decisions at the right time.

My journey to evaluate my own personality started during my childhood through my parents and continues even today. I went through various hardships and many ups and downs in my life. At each step, I learned how to bring out my own personality, and I had a knack for immediately correcting myself to further refine my abilities.

I would like you, the reader, to assess yourself using the following outline, to see where you stand today and how you can learn to bring out your skill set to improve your leadership abilities and potentially become a natural-born leader. The following assessment tool will serve as a guideline for you.

Self-Assessment Tool	Strongly Disagree	Disagree	Neutral	Agree	Strongly Agree	Response
I have a foundation, background, or base knowledge about the organization I work for or about a task that I am trying to accomplish.	1	2	3	4	5	
I have a clear vision in mind when setting out to do something.	1	2	3	4	5	
I am insightful.	1	2	3	4	5	
I have self-confidence when making decisions.	1	2	3	4	5	
I perform daily tasks without expecting any external reward(s) (i.e. money, gifts, praise).	1	2	3	4	5	
I have integrity.	1	2	3	4	5	
Others trust my decisions.	1	2	3	4	5	
I seek long-term gratification.	1	2	3	4	5	
I stay calm during stressful situations.	1	2	3	4	5	
I have fearlessness in making critical decisions.	1	2	3	4	5	
I demonstrate genuine concern or empathy over the suffering of others.	1	2	3	4	5	
I am able to effectively communicate with others.	1	2	3	4	5	
I have strong listening and observation skills.	1	2	3	4	5	
I am willing to give up my time for others.	1	2	3	4	5	
I approach tasks from new perspectives and ask questions.	1	2	3	4	5	
I can say, "I don't know" situationally.	1	2	3	4	5	
I see the glass of water half full.	1	2	3	4	5	
I treat others equally and with respect.	1	2	3	4	5	
I am generous.	1	2	3	4	5	
I obtain happiness or pleasure when completing a difficult task.	1	2	3	4	5	
Total Score						

Scoring Guidlines				
0-20	21-40	41-60	61-80	81-100
Not a Natural Born Leader <————————> Natural Born Leader				

Awards and Honors

The following awards and award nominations were not my desire, but due to the hospital administration's decision to nominate for various awards in Saudi Arabia and USA.

- Nominated in 2016 Lifetime Achievement Award with the Association of Physicians of Pakistani Descent in North America (APPNA).

National Federal Recognition

- The Chicago Federal Executive Board 2016, Finalist, Management Excellence Award
- Nominated Jesse Brown Spirit Award, 2010 to 2016
- The Chicago Federal Executive Board Nominee for the 2015 Exceptional Professional Employee of the Year Award
- Received Several Special Contribution, Monitoring, and Incentive Awards between 2005 to 2016
- Nominated for the category of Outstanding Team Award in Chicago metropolitan area for Chicago Federal Employee of the Year in 2009, 2012, and 2013
- Nominated Service to America Medal in 2006, 2007, and 2008. The Partnership and Atlantic Media Company—publisher of Government Executive, National Journal and The Atlantic—created the Service to America Medals program in 2002 to publicly recognize outstanding federal employees who dedicate their lives to making a difference, which encourages a new generation to join the federal workforce. Nearly six hundred deserving public servants (out of ten million federal work forces) were nominated in the years 2006, 2007, and 2008. With so many compelling and inspiring stories, it was a real challenge to narrow the field to only thirty finalists. Dr. Salar should take pride in knowing that Dr. Salar's effort and accomplishments are recognized and appreciated.

- Chicago Federal Employee of the Year 2006, Winner for the Program Specialist Category.

Recognition in the USA

- Employee of the Year 1997, Edgewater Medical Center, Chicago, Illinois, due to successfully and independently completing and saving several thousands of dollars for the hospital.

International Recognition

- 1993—Certificate of Thanks and Recognition for Excellent Performance and Best Patient Care under Ministry of Health (MOH), Saudi Arabia
- 1992—Certificate for Enhancing Hospital Reputation through High Standards under MOH, Saudi Arabia
- 1990—Certificate for Excellent Job Performance and Best Patient Care under MOH, Saudi Arabia
- 1989—Best Hospital Employee under MOH, Saudi Arabia

Index

H

hajj, 75–76

happiness, xiii, xvii, xli, xlvii–xlviii, 9, 19, 23, 25, 59, 61, 67, 72, 77, 79, 115–16

hard work, 6, 8–9, 55, 63, 113, 118

honesty, 6, 11, 23, 25, 80, 118

hospital director, xlv, xlvii, 26–27, 41–46, 49, 51, 53, 55, 79, 94, 107

Human Research Protection Program (HRPP), 108–12

hypochondriasis, 74

I

institutional review board (IRB), 109, 111, 113

intuition, xvii, xxxvii, 17, 21, 24–25, 33–35, 53, 55, 59, 68–71, 74, 76–77, 96–101, 106, 120

Islamabad, Pakistan, 54

J

Jesse Brown Veterans Affairs Medical Center (JBVAMC), xliii, 61, 106–13, 116

Jinnah Postgraduate Medical Center, 38, 95

job, xxii–xxiii, xlvii, 7, 11, 21, 23, 25, 28–29, 56, 58–59, 72–73, 84–85, 109, 111–12, 114–16

Joint Commission Accreditation Hospital Organization (JCAHO), 108

K

Karachi, Pakistan, xliii, 1–3, 6–7, 35, 37–41, 43, 45, 48–49, 54–56, 58–59, 62, 72, 78, 95, 99–100

Karachi Psychiatric Hospital, 38–41, 45, 102

Khan, Faraz Ahmed, 49

Khan, Mukhtar Ahmed, xxviii, xlii–xliii, 2–4, 6–8, 13, 15–16, 54, 58, 93, 98–99

Khan, Noorjehan, xvi, xlvii, 1–2, 8–10, 14–15, 48

Khan, Rubina, 48–49

Khan, Saad Ahmed, 49

Khan, Salar Ahmed, iv, xv–xvi, xix, xxvii, xxxvii, 39, 42, 44–45, 53, 73, 122

King Fahad Hospital, 93, 96

L

leaders, xxiv, xxvii–xxix, xxxiii–xxxv, xli–xliii, xlv, xlviii–xlix, 6, 20–22, 25–32, 36–37, 62–63, 65–66, 91–92, 104, 114

leadership, xi, xv–xvii, xix–xxi, xxvii, xxxiii–xxxv, xli–xliii, xlv, xlix, 8–9, 20, 27–30, 35, 47–48, 61–66, 106

leadership intuition, 17, 27–28, 32, 59, 106, 113

leadership qualities, xvii, xxviii–xxix, xxxiii, 9, 66, 118

communication, 19, 24–25, 27, 53, 55, 68, 83–84, 113, 120

compassion, xxxviii, 11, 17, 19, 26, 33, 53, 57, 68, 102–3, 109

composure, xxxvii, 19, 25–27, 33, 55, 68, 75, 87, 91–92, 94, 106, 108

courage, xxxviii, xlii, 11, 19, 26, 33, 46, 67–68, 100–101

insightfulness, xvii, xxxvii, 19, 25–27, 33, 53, 55, 68, 70–72, 74, 106, 108

integrity, 55, 68, 80, 82, 120

intrinsic motivation, xxxiv, xlvi, 6, 16, 19, 25, 57, 60, 68, 77, 79, 107

open-mindedness, xxxvii, 19, 26–27, 33, 35, 55, 68, 94, 97, 100, 111

optimism, xxxviii, 5, 19, 26, 33, 65, 68, 79, 90, 103–4

patience, xxxvii, 19, 25, 33, 68, 87–89, 91

sacrifice, xxxvii, 7, 18–19, 25–26, 33, 68, 78, 84, 86–87, 114, 118

self-confidence, xvi–xvii, xxiii, xxviii, xxxiv–xxxv, xxxvii, xlvi–xlvii, xlix, 2–4, 9, 18–19, 21–22, 25–27, 31–37, 70–72, 106

Los Angeles, California, 58

Lucknow, India, 8

lymphoma, 101

M

Mecca, 75–76

meningitis, 38, 98

mind-set, xliii, xlviii, 27, 32, 63–65, 67, 107, 115

Ministry of Health (MOH), 23, 41, 46–50, 54, 72, 86, 116, 123

Minna (city), 76

motivation, xxiii, 9, 11, 30, 77, 98

mutanjan (rice dish), 8

N

National Committee for Quality Assurance (NCQA), 109–10

natural-born leader (NBL), xvi–xvii, xx–xxi, xxiii–xxiv, xxxv–xxxvi, xli–xlii, xlv–xlix, 13–14, 17, 20–24, 26, 28, 30–32, 63–65, 112–14, 118–20

NED Engineering College, 7

O

observation skills, 25, 99, 121

Office of Research Oversight (ORO), 108–9, 113

O'Hare International Airport, 59

Ojah Institute of Chest Diseases, 38

P

pneumothorax, 44

psychiatry, 33, 38–41, 45, 53

R

Rizvi, Syed Adib Hasan, 37, 72–74

S

Saudi Arabia, xiii, xvi, xxxv, xxxvii, xliii, xlvii, 7, 23, 26–27, 40–41, 47–50, 53–58, 79, 106, 122–23

Shahid (student of Salar), 77, 79

Sind Institute of Urology and Transplantation (SIUT), 37

standard operating procedure (SOP), 50, 52, 109

storytelling, xvii, 10, 12, 14, 119

success, 1, 4, 6, 8–9, 36–37, 54, 64–68, 84, 103, 107, 114, 118

Syed, Shaukat, 96

T

tabula rasa, 94

Telephone and Telegraph (T&T) Department, 7

time management, 2

U

United States, xlvii, 7, 30, 37, 40, 54, 58, 62, 78, 99, 116

United States Agency of International Development, 58

University of Illinois at Chicago (UIC), 61, 107–8, 111–13

University of Karachi, 38

urology, 37, 72–75

V

visceral leishmaniasis, 85

W

weaknesses, xlviii, 16, 30, 47, 72
Wolff-Parkinson-White   syndrome
    (WPW), 96–97